THE
BOOK
OF
KEHLS

THE
BOOK
OF
KEHLS

CHRISTINE KEHL O'HAGAN

ST. MARTIN'S GRIFFIN   NEW YORK

www.stmartins.com

Library of Congress Cataloging-in-Publication Data

O'Hagan, Christine
    The book of Kehls / Christine Kehl O'Hagan.
        p. cm.
    ISBN 0-312-32955-5 (hc)
    ISBN 0-312-32956-3 (pbk)
    EAN 978-0-312-32956-3
    1. Duchenne muscular dystrophy—Patients—New York
(State)—New York—Biography. 2. Kehl family. 3. Irish
American families—New York (State)—New York. I. Title.

RJ482.D78 O37 2005
362.196'748'0092—dc22
[B]
                                                    2004056474

First St. Martin's Griffin Edition: February 2006

10 9 8 7 6 5 4 3 2 1

For my son, Patrick

ACKNOWLEDGMENTS

I'M GRATEFUL TO MY HUSBAND, PATRICK, WHO shelters me, body and soul, and to my sister, Pam, who gives me courage.

My brother-in-law, Charlie, is grace under pressure, and my nephews, Chris and Jason, teach me to persevere.

My daughter-in-law, Nicole, is the daughter of my heart, and Alanna, the granddaughter of my dreams.

For over forty years, Ruth Faranda has been the "one true friend" my young mother once wished for me. Doreen Robbins Hatter and Diane Lavery were the true friends I once wished for Jamie.

To everyone who helped us in our struggle—Elizabeth and Angel Rodriguez, Tony and Jimmy Faranda, Sue and Ray Lani, Janie and Paul Cisek, Paula and Ed Cossack, Roseanne, Bill, Erik Schreuder, Susan O'Connell, David O'Connell, Kathryn Moeller—thank you. You meant more to us than you could ever know.

Once again, my agent, Ann Rittenberg, encouraged me—despite the commas. From the beginning, Dori Weintraub, my editor, heard what I was trying to say. Mickey Pearlman is both dear friend and "rabbi," and Saralee Rosenberg, friend and treasure. With special thanks to Jerry Lewis.

"At once the lost boys—but where are they?
They are no longer there.
Rabbits could not have disappeared more quickly. . . ."

PETER PAN
J. M. Barrie

THE
BOOK
OF
KEHLS

PROLOGUE

Although we didn't realize it at the time, May 19, 1998, in the ICU of Long Island's Stony Brook Hospital, was the last evening that my husband Patrick and I would ever be together with both our sons, Pat Jr., who was twenty-six and newly married, and Jamie, who was twenty-four, and in the last stages of Duchenne muscular dystrophy.

The signs that our time together was almost up were everywhere, if only we'd looked. At home, Jamie had been so quiet, spending most of his day staring out the living-room window, like someone yearning to leave the party for the comfort of his own warm bed. (Later on, I'll realize that we'd been lousy hosts, wouldn't get his coat, kept telling him jokes, and refilling his glass.) He was down to sixty-seven pounds. He'd asked me—hypothetically speaking, of course—how many people would come to his funeral. ("Ten," he said. "Two hundred plus," I said, never imagining how it would feel to see Janie and Paul, our former neighbors, who'd driven all the way from

Maryland, or Jimmy Willmer, from Princeton, New Jersey, although he was waiting for a new heart, and supposed to stay close to home. He never made it. Only three months later, Jimmy was gone too. And then there were Jamie's grade-school teachers who'd stood together in the back of the room, like some surreal Open School Night. Two hundred people, and then some.)

And now, Jamie was in bad shape. He couldn't get off the vent, couldn't breathe on his own, could barely eat, could hardly swallow. Not the whipped-cream pastries from the New Milford, Connecticut, "patisserie" that my sister, Pam, had bought, packed in a cooler, and driven three hours to offer him, not the spoonful of custard Patrick Sr. tried to feed him, not Patrick Jr.'s strawful of warm tea. Not the bit of scrambled egg I tried to slip into his mouth, vent and all, when the doctors urged him to eat, and then left the room without telling me quite how to go about feeding him. (For the rest of my life, I'll wonder if he'd aspirated that bit of egg, and that's what finally did him in.) At any rate, he wasn't taking enough food or water to keep him alive.

We knew that, and yet at the same time, we refused to know it.

In my loud, semihysterical hospital voice, I assured him that he'd be home again before he knew it, back to his television and his crossword puzzles, the tiny life I wanted him to keep accepting. I told him it was "only another pneumonia," "only another ambulance ride," "only another hospital tune-up." The Duchenne muscular dystrophy I gave him was also destroying the life I gave him, but where there's life, there's hope, and I wasn't giving up.

If I'd known that he had only hours left to live, and he was about to die in my arms—the same freckled, jiggly, middle-aged arms where my mother had suddenly died not even a year before—I'd have bolted from that hospital room, raced down the seventeen flights of stairs, and run out onto Nicoll's Road, ripping off my clothes, pulling out my hair, and quite possibly hurling myself in front of a truck. I'd held my mother tighter than I'd ever held anyone before, but her life flew out from under my fingertips, and she died anyway, bang, just like that. So much for the control I thought I had over things. "At least she didn't have to bury another boy with muscular dystrophy," her friends said, and that was true enough. Her grandsons all outlived her. But what about me, and what about Pam? Richie had only been gone a year when we found out that Jamie, and Pam and Charlie's sons, Christopher and Jason, had muscular dystrophy. We didn't think about how unbearable it might have been for Mom, no longer a muscular dystrophy mother to one boy, but a muscular dystrophy grandmother to three. We never thought that maybe she'd had enough. Instead, we thought more about ourselves, the new muscular dystrophy mothers, and how much we still needed her. Though Mom was well into her seventies and lived in Queens, she got to Long Island and Connecticut whenever the boys were in the hospital, coming through the door with deli sandwiches, rosary beads, Kleenex, and optimism. When Chris was recovering from surgery, she'd even taken a yellow cab from Roosevelt Avenue in Jackson Heights to Pam's house in the foot of the Berkshire mountains. When Jamie was lying in that hospital bed for what turned out to be the last time, I needed her more than ever.

But now she was gone.

Alpha and omega bookends, the future and the past, my mother and my son.

When Jamie was diagnosed, he was only seven years old—the Catholic Church's "age of reason." The doctor told us that though there weren't any guarantees, he'd "probably" live to see sixteen. We never told Jamie that—we were afraid he'd believe it. Each of his September twentieth birthdays—when he had more candles on his cake, perhaps, but was less able to blow them out—were bittersweet victories. And now, despite our vigilance, beyond our control, the new nurse who came to our house never told us she had a cold. When Jamie caught it, it became pneumonia. A pneumonia with fangs, more vicious than the others, for at sixty-seven pounds, he had no reserve. Though there had been a dozen others, the last pneumonia was the killer.

For the first time, Jamie's doctors offered him "options." They could do a trach to ease his breathing problems permanently, and they could put a feeding tube into his belly temporarily—only they didn't call it a "feeding tube," they called it a "button," a snub-nosed freckle of a word. Who doesn't love a button? They said it would be "easy" to do, and yes, they could even do it under local anesthesia. But there was a caveat—if things started to go "badly," then Jamie might have to be intubated anyway. And with respiratory muscles as weak as his, he might never be "extubated." "No trach," Jamie said, "no 'tube,' no 'button.' I don't want to live on machines." He agreed to go to the hospital only to be weaned from the vent, for observation, for IV fluids. He agreed to try the nasal feedings the doctors halfheartedly suggested. But when we got to the hospital, he couldn't be weaned from anything. He couldn't come off the vent, not even for a second, and he couldn't tolerate the nasal feedings. There was nothing else the doctors could offer. In medicine, as in so many other things, "options" aren't always choices.

It was springtime on Long Island, and the view from Jamie's big window an E. M. Forster delight. Like so many babies who start out blond, the treetops below us were pale, a delicate, soft green. In the distance, I could see a silvery ribbon of the Long Island Sound, and a few tiny sailboats. At dusk, the nursery-pink sky was cheery and encouraging. So much life erupted on the other side of that glass that surely there seemed to be enough for Jamie. For months, "choose life" was the subliminal, Vulcan mind-meld message I'd been sending him while we were sitting side by side (wheelchair for him, rocking chair for me) in the living room watching TV. And I told myself that Jamie was listening. Though he'd been under seventy pounds for a long time, and had been sick over and over again, he always rebounded. It's only another pneumonia, I told myself, stop making it such a big, dramatic event. The pink sky almost had me convinced that we'd take him home yet again. Another day or so of antibiotics, another day or so on the vent, and I was fairly certain he'd turn the corner. Whether he wanted to come home yet again was something I didn't want to think about. Especially when he asked each of us, in turn, if it was "okay to stop trying." "Of course," we said, hearing his question, and not listening to our own answers.

When it was night, and the view disappeared, I flicked the light switch, and Jamie's room turned a glowing, warm yellow, as if the sun were rising from behind his bed. Scott, Jamie's first male nurse ever, popped in to introduce himself. He was short, peppy, enthusiastically freckled. He looked like the young Mickey Rooney, as if he were on his way to find Judy Garland and put on a show in the barn. He called Jamie "Sport," and "Champ," and "Buddy." Although we'd told Jamie that it was okay to stop trying, I didn't think any of us meant it—how could we?—and Scott seemed to be on our side. Or perhaps it was only my side. Both Patricks, sitting mutely in their orange plastic chairs, staring at their hands, looked up at Scott, watched him wave his clipboard, listened politely to his "game plan." Gatorade, Jell-O, a stronger and more powerful antibiotic, the respiratory "team." Although we had a refrigerator full of Gatorade and Jell-O at home, although Jamie had been on two powerful antibiotics for a week, although I'd been doing his respiratory therapy for years, I was so exhausted and frightened that I was weirdly exhilarated by this cheery new outlook, this tiny bit of hope, as if it offered something new. I wanted to go over and pick up Scott, put him on my shoulders, run with him around the happy yellow room. At the very least, I thought, it might make Jamie laugh. If Scott was the team mascot, then I was the cheerleader. The two of us grinned at Patrick and Pat, who stared at the speckled tile floor, and at Jamie who slept. Or pretended to sleep. With Jamie, I was never sure. When he was younger, and in the hospital, and intern "clowns" with grimy, oversize daisies stuck in their lapels and dachshund balloons in their latex-gloved hands wandered into his room, Jamie thought it was funny to throw himself back on the pillows, let his head loll on his right shoulder, drool, and pretend to be comatose.

Trust me—it isn't easy to make small talk with a clown.

When Scott looked up from fiddling with the oxygen valve alongside Jamie's bed, and promised me a "wonderful" chair so I could get some sleep, I nearly cried. I yearned for too many impossibilities—my mother's cool hands on my forehead, Jamie breathing on his own, my stomach settling down. The "wonderful" chair, with an hour of sleep tucked inside, was at least a possibility, and I was overjoyed. Unwashed, unfed, unslept, I'd been at the hospital for a very long time. My head pounded so hard that I felt giddy. I told Scott that I wanted that chair, and I wanted it now. (Later on, I was shocked when Patrick Sr. told me that while I was carrying on about the chair, he and Pat had seen Scott raise Jamie's oxygen intake to the highest setting. Although I was the one who'd obsessed over every painstaking bit of Jamie's most eensy-weensy care, I was so tired I simply hadn't noticed.)

As soon as Scott left, Patrick and Pat stood up. Though Pat and Nicole lived in Connecticut, whenever Jamie was sick, Pat came home to Long Island. After being out of work, Patrick Sr. had just started a new job. Although his boss was under-standing, and Patrick left early, he had to be at work most of the day. Patrick Jr.'s job was more flexible. On Jamie's last day,

Pat had been with us since the early morning. Since Jamie was seven years old, his early death was the first thing I thought about in the morning, and the last thing at night. If losing Jamie was inevitable, and the thing I feared most in the world, Pat being alone with Jamie when it happened was a close second. I didn't want Pat, the muscular dystrophy survivor, to bear that burden too, spending the rest of his life wondering if he might somehow have saved him. Saving Jamie—or not saving Jamie—was my domain. And so while I probably should have, and later would wonder if my zealous care of Jamie might have elbowed Pat and Patrick and who knows who else out of the way, when Jamie was in the hospital, I never left the boys alone. When the sparse-haired social worker beckoned me to a small room at the end of the corridor, sat me down, and told me how sick Jamie really was, I stared at her pink scalp, thinking of bad permanent waves, and caustic hair dyes, and tried not to listen. *You don't know my son,* I thought, *you've never seen him pull through. You've never seen the smiles on the doctors' and nurses' faces when they see him back in their waiting rooms.* "Thank you," I said, cutting short her sad-eyed spiel. I slammed the door when I left the room. I couldn't get away from her fast enough.

On Patrick's wedding day, Jamie had told me that he loved Patrick more than anyone in the world. "Even me?" I'd asked, surprised and a little hurt. I was the one who'd been at Jamie's side night and day, his lifelong, constant companion, determined to make him laugh, determined to share with him whatever I thought he might find, if not fascinating, then interesting, even if that meant eye-rolling (him) and non sequiturs (me)—what the hell, I sometimes got him to laugh. And when he did, it was as if I'd won the lottery. I so wanted Jamie to forgive me. Whatever it was that might give him the "oomph" to live, I was eager to try. And sometimes it worked. A good movie, or when he could still swallow, a nice restaurant, or even a funny book propped up on the book stand of his hospital tray. All of those "yeses" were tiny, perhaps, but piled on top of one another, they added up to twenty-four years.

But then there were the more recent weeks when he didn't smile, when everything hurt him, when he wouldn't even look up at me. Though Diane, his last nurse, didn't let him get away with it, there were days when he didn't want to get out of bed. Sometimes, after she left, I put him back into bed, climbed onto the mattress, and spooned with him, both of us on our right sides, my left arm around his tiny waist, my hand resting on his heart—as if, by touch, I could heal him. "Well, yeah," Jamie had laughed, his blue eyes sparkling, "I love Pat more," he said, and I hit him on the head with the kaiser roll I had in my hand. It took everything Jamie had to be Patrick's best man, including throwing up all over poor Diane right before the ceremony, but he carried it off. After Jamie's toast, when he told a hundred and fifty people that Nicole, his former classmate, was the sister he'd always wanted, there wasn't a dry eye in the house. Just like the rest of us, Jamie knew how perfect Nicole was for Pat.

Although I knew that Patrick and Pat were hungry and tired, they were the back-up and support team and when they were ready to leave, I was scared. I couldn't get Jamie to say much, but earlier, when Pat dropped his pants and mooned him, Jamie had actually laughed. Thus encouraged, Pat then stumbled over the orange plastic chair, and into the garbage pail, and Jamie had laughed some more. "Good night, Ugly," Pat said, bending over Jamie, staring into his eyes. "Shut up, Idiot," was Jamie's response, the last exchange they'd ever have. "Better tomorrow," Patrick commanded, rubbing Jamie's hair. "Yup," Jamie said, sounding for all the world exactly like John Wayne. Then father and son kissed the top of my head, and left. Standing in the doorway, I watched them walk toward the elevator. Side by side, with Patrick's massive arm around Pat's massive shoulder, they barely fit in the corridor. Their heads almost touched the ceiling. The next night, between them, they'd drink an ocean of beer, and though the house would be full of people, they'd stand in the driveway together with their arms around each other like a couple of bears. *One gene,* I thought, as I watched them from the back, and it could have been so different.

Scott came back with a tray. More Jell-O, more Gatorade. Behind him, an orderly carried the "wonderful" chair. When I realized it was the same white chair they'd brought me all the other times, I was ready to cry. Low-slung, mesh, it was a terrible chair with a bar that cut into the base of my spine. I sank into it anyway, too tired to sleep, too tired to stay awake. In three seconds, my back began to tingle.

Please God, I prayed, dusting off my old, three-sentence, ICU mantra.

Just a little more time.

I will do whatever it takes to bring him home again.

I'm not yet ready to give him up.

Then I remembered something I'd recently read: "the answer to most prayers is no," and then I looked at him, in yet one more ICU bed, listened to his moans and gasps, watched his struggle to breathe, and that three-sentence mantra felt outdated, selfish, wrong. For whatever reason, I'd finished looking down at Jamie, and then up at Pat, trying to novocaine myself, trying not to feel. The effort had suddenly become too much. When I was with my two sons, my heart felt ready to explode. "What might have been" was always with me, a continual ache behind my eyes. Poor Jamie, poor Pat, poor us. Patrick and I had looked at our beautiful firstborn son, and because we were foolish, reckless, and so terribly young, we thought that Duchenne muscular dystrophy was too busy with my brother Richie to bother with Patrick Jr., and for a while, we were right. But then it happened to Jamie, and all that he has been denied was killing him—and killing us too. Although a night's sleep is nothing to someone who can barely move, we hadn't had an unbroken night's sleep in over a decade. Sometimes, when I looked at Jamie, he was already staring at me. "What?" I'd ask, heart pounding, afraid of the answer, but Jamie never said any more, just slowly shook his head. I thought it'd be easier for him to say what was on his mind if he weren't looking at me, so I stood next to his wheelchair, rubbed his back, and waited. And waited. But he said nothing, just kept shaking his head.

This May Tuesday night, for the first time, as I watched Jamie struggle, I could clearly see that it was simply costing him much to live, and so I put my head back on the white mesh chair, with its flat, attached "pillow," and imagined picking him up, his grown-up head fitting neatly into the crook of my arm, and placing him into what I imagined to be the puffy white hand of God. "Whatever God wants," is what my mother-in-law said, or "Jamie is God's child too."

God's kid, "Jerry's Kid," and my kid.

My own kid, and I prayed for his hard life to end.

The "respiratory team" turned out to be an overly made-up young woman with a put-upon attitude, and far too many rings. She clanged as she tapped Jamie's small chest, unenthusiastically loosening secretions about half as effectively as I'd been doing for weeks, months, years, centuries. Fighting sleep, I watched her, and I was anxious for her to leave, so I could do his respiratory therapy again, putting more effort into it, despite the worst headache of my life, and the fear that I was about to throw up into the garbage pail next to the bed. Though the glass was probably shatterproof (and would no doubt have made my headache much worse), I briefly considered jumping through the big window. Instead of admitting that my son was dying, I simply told myself that I was no good at hospitals, that I'd been in far too many of them. ("Poor you," whispers the sarcastic voice of wicked Sister Bernice, my Catholic schoolgirl conscience. Usually she whispers "all for Jesus," but that's only when I'm emptying the urinal or cleaning the bedpan. "What about Jamie?" she asked. "Maybe he's been in far too many hospital *beds*.")

Yet, whenever Jamie was admitted, I was the one the clerks seemed worried about. They handed me Advil from their own stash, and lukewarm water in tiny, pleated, paper cups. Though at the time Jamie was usually gasping for air, he was the one who answered the questions, and I was the one who was shaking so badly, I couldn't say a word. "Just hold my hand, Mom," Jamie said, and I did. In those tiny admitting offices, it looked to all the world as if I were soothing him, but it was really the other way around.

Every time I looked at the monitor above the bed, and saw that Jamie's oxygen saturation was 90 percent or better, it was a gift, and I was grateful. I'd prayed for an end to Jamie's suffering but maybe "no" was God's answer to that prayer too. *Maybe,* I thought, *it's just not time;* but then the machines suddenly alarmed, and the numbers plummeted. I leapt to my feet, and Scott raced into the room. "False alarm," he said and smiled, and I sat down before I fell down. "It's just that Jamie's mouth opens when he sleeps," he said, and handed me a Velcro chin strap to make the mask covering his nose tighter. I got up, pulled the chin strap snug, and sat back down. Then he started moaning, louder and louder, and dear God, I thought he was just uncomfortable. He was so thin that his bones poked through his flesh, and the mattress was so hard. From the bathroom, I got towels, rolled them up, stuck them behind his back, in between his knees, and then he was quiet. I was asleep before I sat down. All I wanted was an hour, one lousy hour. When the moaning began again, I woke up, and turned into a crazy woman, jumping up from the chair, livid, flushed, furious. *"Goddamn it!"* I shouted, middle of the night or not, ICU or not, *"I can't be doing this night after night!*"—can you imagine—and then when I looked down at him again, my tirade fizzled out, as if it had belonged to someone else, and God's grace kicked in. Nearly ten pounds when he was born, and sixty-seven pounds at age twenty-four. I'd given Jamie life, perhaps, but inadvertently had taken away breath. I pulled the Velcro strap away from his face, and tossed it onto the hospital tray, next to the watery container of Jell-O and warm bottle of Gatorade, and shoved the whole tray across the room. I decided not to sit down and risk falling asleep again. When the machine alarmed again, I bent over and softly closed his mouth. "Mommy's here," I whispered, as if he were four rather than twenty-four. "Mommy's here," I repeated, rubbing his arms and legs, trying to think of what to do next.

But there was nothing to do next.

"You know," a smiling Indian doctor wearing a purple and gold sari had said on the day he was admitted, "he just might make it," but now, when she passed his door, she no longer waved and smiled, but instead, kept her head down and stared at the floor. Too many people were staring at the floor. The "mights" were quitting on him, along with the "shoulds," and were leaving with all the possibilities.

Earlier in the day, even before Patrick Jr. had gotten to the hospital, Jamie had suddenly begged me to call slim, young, boyish Father M., whom Jamie had been to see. "About the trach?" I asked Jamie, "about the 'button'?" but he wouldn't tell me. "I just need to speak to him for a few minutes," he said, slowly, hesitantly. He had to pace his words to the hissing of the vent. "I think I'd feel better." Relieved, I dialed the phone, for it was exactly what I would have done in Jamie's place. I was overjoyed to hear Father M. answer the phone himself, and while Jamie stared at me, wide-eyed, unbearably frightened looking, I explained it all. The trach, the button. Please Father, I begged, please come. Though the rectory is less than thirty minutes away from the hospital, Father M. said he was sorry, he just couldn't make it. No, not even for a few minutes. He was sorry. No further explanation. It just wasn't possible. "Can't he talk to me on the phone?" Father M. asked. "No, Father," I said, "he's struggling too hard to breathe." Then we hung up, for there was nothing more to say. "Maybe he's got something more important to do," I said to Jamie, but Jamie ignored my sarcasm, and just shrugged. "Yeah, maybe," he said.

But then, about an hour later, Father K., the hospital chaplain, came to Jamie's room. "What took you so long?" I almost asked, for though I'd never seen him before, and nobody told us he was on his way, I was expecting him. I'd been around serious illness long enough to know that no matter how simple or profound, *yes* is always on the heels of every *no*. When you need them most, someone always shows up. It's almost as if they give off a certain spark, like an electrical charge, that's invisible to the eye, perhaps, but not to the heart, and gives just enough light to bring you to where you need to go next. Father K. was taller, older, more substantial looking than the ethereal Father M. He waited patiently at Jamie's bedside, but Jamie was shy, didn't know him, and said nothing. When

Father K. left the room, Jamie sent me after him. "I need a blessing," Jamie explained when Father K. came back into the room. "The Blessing of the Sick," as it's now called, somewhat vaguely, is not the simple, unequivocal, Last Rites. "Do you feel better?" I asked Jamie, after Father K. had left. He closed his eyes, sighed, and nodded: *yes.*

One of the intensive care doctors came to Jamie's room. Had we changed our minds about the trach, or the "button"? I looked down at Jamie, he looked up at me, and I began to cry. "Look at you," the disgusted-looking doctor said, his upper lip in an Elvis sneer. There was no spark coming anywhere from him, only a dull, matte finish. He had one long, coal-black "unibrow" in which a fire of red eczema burned. "You need a Valium," he hissed, and stalked out of the room with me in hot pursuit. "What is the moral and ethical thing to do here?" I practically shouted, and the nurses at their station looked up. He didn't answer me. He sat down and stared at the folder in front of him. I wanted to grab his tie, pull him from the chair, and throw him on the floor, stomping out the fire in his eyebrow with my sneaker. I was furious with him, furious with Father M., furious with myself for taking such a chance in the first place. Jamie was too normal, too sweet, too polite, too nice for what was being asked of him. Morals? Ethics? We took it for granted that the second baby would be as healthy as the first. We gave more thought to buying a sofa, and a TV. To me, no risk a young person takes is beyond my comprehension.

"What would you do if this were *your* child?" I demanded.

"When is it giving up, and when is it letting go?" It's the age of technological miracles, yet none of us knows the answer to that one. At first, he said nothing. Then, finally, without looking up, he said, "That's an unfair question." Unlike Jamie's former doctor, a woman with a handicapped child of her own, he didn't put down his pen, get up, come around from the nurses' station and embrace me. Instead, he began writing in his folder, the son of a bitch, and I cried until I had no tears left. Then I wiped my face on my sleeve, and went back to Jamie's room, where he seemed, finally, to be asleep. I walked to the big window to compose myself. At night, this part of Long Island is pitch black. There is no view. On Long Island, we can see everything during the day, but nothing at night. When you look out the window on a Long Island night, all you can see is yourself. And there I was: a middle-aged woman in glasses staring back, and behind me, underneath those tubes and blankets, what muscular dystrophy had left of my son. *Bring on the wide-screen TVs.*

In front of the hospital was the taxi stand, where two taxis were waiting. I only needed one, I thought, and I was only thirty minutes from my own bed. I'd just go to the desk, tell Scott I was leaving, and I'd be back in a few hours. "You *left* him?" an incredulous Patrick or Pat would say, jumping up the minute they heard my key in the door. "I was too tired to do him any good," I'd explain, but it sounded lame, even to me. I could feel Sister Bernice breathing down the back of my neck. She was dumbstruck, horrified. We never left Jamie in the hospital by himself. He couldn't move, couldn't ring for the nurse, and his voice was so weak, he'd never be heard. Patrick and I usually took turns sitting up all night. Patrick stayed one night, I stayed the next, but this time, there was the new job, and no sense in both of us being exhausted. Maybe I didn't want Patrick Sr. to be alone with him when it happened either. He was a good man who had been through too much.

I didn't want Valium. I merely wanted one night's sleep in my own bed, and if I couldn't have that, then I thought I'd like hemlock, cyanide, or a loaded pistol if I only knew how to use it. I couldn't leave Jamie, and I wouldn't leave him, sleep be damned. The night before, I'd slept for thirty minutes on a dirty red plastic love seat by the telephones, where I'd opened my eyes once and had seen a wild-haired man in a torn flannel shirt with a roll of toilet paper on his thumb staring at me from the doorway. I was too tired to care. In the state I was in, rape and even murder would have only been diversions.

"You'll have the rest of your life to sleep," Sister Bernice reminded me. "All for Jesus."

In the room next to Jamie was an elderly woman who'd had a stroke. "There's nothing we can do for her," Scott whispered. I was grateful he didn't say "either." Her blond, middle-aged daughters were with her, just waiting for her to pass. They looked like biblical women, wrapped in white cotton blankets against exhaustion, probably, and the hospital's chill. For a minute, when I looked up, and saw them standing in the doorway of Jamie's room, I thought I'd imagined them. Their soft, kind faces, their sad blue eyes. I decided that even if they were hallucinations, I was grateful for the company—more of those sparks—and I thanked them for the very real blueberry muffin and hot cup of tea they brought me. In our loneliest moments, the universe provides.

When it was true dawn, bluish and gray, a tall black nurse came into Jamie's room to take blood. His veins were tiny, and so she had to take arterial blood from his ankle, always a tricky endeavor. She stood on one side of the bed and I stood on the other and we just stared at each other. *It's going to be alright,* her big dark eyes said, and I nodded in response. At Suffolk Community College, it was the black kids, time and again, who went out of their way to hold doors for Jamie, who pulled his motorized wheelchair out of the campus shrubbery, who stopped to pat his shoulder and say hello. When he needed help, the black kids were the ones Jamie always approached. He said they never looked the other way. The nurse fussed with the needle, and because I couldn't stand to see one more needle pierce this child's pale flesh, I went outside, glad to see the next-door daughters standing in front of their mother's room, one daughter asking the other one why it had been Mom rather than Dad, when he was "such a nasty old man." She wasn't trying to be funny, but I was so tired, I laughed anyway. I was relieved when she smiled, and clearly hadn't taken offense.

When it was my turn, I told the sisters that Jamie had muscular dystrophy, the Jerry Lewis Telethon disease, something I must have said a thousand times, and no, he wasn't born with it, which isn't quite true. He *was* born with it. It just didn't show itself for six years. To say that he was born with muscular dystrophy makes people ask if anyone else in the family had muscular dystrophy and that's when I would like to disappear. My brother, my nephews, I say, and then, when the jaws drop, I'm "outed" as the foolish, careless, callous person I fear myself to be. To say that Jamie was born with muscular dystrophy makes his glorious, red-haired, "normal" babyhood even more of a loss, and before I know it, I'm remembering the struggle he had with the school bus steps, and the feeling of hope sputtering in my heart—and I was just too tired to go there. It was easier to pretend that MD had just fallen out of the sky.

I told the sisters that Jamie had graduated from the community college, that he was a writer who'd just published an article in a national magazine, that he had a lot of guts. All true. My ingrained Irishness that tried to sweeten the sorry tale of muscular dystrophy—so much muscular dystrophy!—with anecdotes, quips, exhausting platitudes, and Oprah-esque moments of the triumphant human spirit that only sometimes seemed moth-eaten, worn-out, rusty. That same ingrained Irishness never mentioned the stress, the exhaustion, the treacherous fighting Sundays when I was standing in front of the bathroom door on a nurse-less Sunday morning screaming at Patrick Sr. to get out of the shower and lift Jamie back into bed, or banging on Patrick Jr.'s door, demanding he get up and give us a hand. It wouldn't be polite to admit that the only way I could get through Jamie's care was by taking as many ten-minute naps as I could, bawling like a toddler when it was time to wake up.

My Irish good manners wouldn't let me talk about any of that.

———

When I noticed one sister holding rosary beads, I told them that Father M. wouldn't come to the hospital, wouldn't even offer an excuse. There's nothing that can't be said in an ICU at six in the morning, no matter how thick the voice, or how sour the breath. They were satisfyingly shocked, and then they wandered off. Before I went back into Jamie's room, I glanced at the monitor above his door, and I noticed the date: May 20, and I began to sweat. September 20 was his birthday. September 20 to May 20. He was such a methodical, organized Virgo that I knew it would be just like him to leave this earth "neat," orderly, Tupperware soul that he was, and before I could think any further, it was as though we were actors in a play, everyone knew their lines, we were all hitting our marks.

The first thing I noticed, while Scott was fussing with the bed linens, was Jamie's unfocused left eye. The blue eyes that so delighted me—me, with a blue-eyed child, can you imagine? I was as proud of those eyes, and thick black eyelashes, as if I'd colored them myself. "Jamie," I crooned, "Jamie, come on now," and I pushed softly at his bearded cheek, leaned over him, close to his face. But his eye wasn't seeing me. At first, I didn't want Scott to see him. Like Jackie Kennedy, hiding the President's bloody head in her lap, I covered Jamie's face with my hand. September 20 to May 20. Oh my God.

But Scott saw him anyway. "His eye," I said, feeling like a Judas, and the room was suddenly filled with buzzers, bells, alarms, and people pushing me out of the way. Two Asian doctors, a small Filipino nurse, a heavy nurse holding a small hammer. "Unresponsive," she said, and I grabbed the phone, and called Patrick. "What do you mean 'unresponsive'?" he yelled, but the alarms kept ringing, and there were more people around Jamie's bed, and I couldn't spend another second on the phone, and so I threw the receiver at Scott, and I heard him tell Patrick that Jamie was "failing" and he'd better come right away. I pushed through the crowd, and back onto his bed. I leaned over him, my hands spread over his small chest, my cheek pressed to his. "I love you, Jamie," I said, "you were the best son, the best brother anyone could ever have. I'm sorry, I'm sorry, I'm sorry," I said, kissing his cheek, pushing the dark hair away from his forehead. The alarms were louder and increasingly more insistent and when it was over, I heard them for a week.

"Please," one of the Asian doctors tugged at my sleeve, "can we intubate? Can we do a trach?" and I shook my head, no, no, no. The decision wasn't hard, just excruciating. In his short life, Jamie hadn't asked for much. He didn't want to live on a machine. No tubes, no cutting. "What can we do?" the doctor asked, standing next to me with his hands palms-up. I looked up at him. "We're going to let him go," I said, "please open the window," and the little nurse did, running halfway across the room. She came back and held one of my shoulders, and the doctor held the other. More strangers, more sparks. If only I could go with him, I thought, my head resting against his heart. Our souls skimming the tops of those baby blond trees, the brilliant, sunlit water, the baby blue sky. He'd been my baby for twenty-four years, and for that moment, I couldn't imagine the "why" of living without him. As the numbers fell lower and lower, I held him tighter and tighter—as uselessly as I'd held my mother. I thought of the *Pieta*—I'd seen it at the World's Fair, in the nineteen-sixties—and I prayed to the Blessed Mother, who had given my mother such solace when my brother died. I hoped she'd give that solace to me.

I pushed everyone away, elbowing someone in green scrubs whose long, dark hair was falling on Jamie's pillow, and I put my face close to his, inhaled deeply, and tried with all my might to catch his pneumonia. His faint breath smelled sweet and clean, like grass and fresh air, as if the process to where he was going, or what he was about to become, had already begun. "Will my husband make it in time?" I asked Scott, who was standing on the other side of the bed.

"He's already gone," Scott said softly, taking the mask from Jamie's face, and that was it. All the years of sleepless nights, guilt, hard work, laughing, the pain and sorrow of it all, it was over, just like that. No more struggling to swallow, no more struggling to breathe. Scott shut down the machines, and the strange eerie silence that's been following me like a stray dog ever since, began.

At the end of his life, Jamie looked much as he had at the beginning, as if all those terrible years had never happened, and he could start again. His old freckles popped out, so bright on his pale face. They reminded me of the surprise mop of red hair he sprouted when he was two, the year he'd won the Toddler Race at Patrick's company picnic. I covered him tightly—he was getting cold. I couldn't bear to close his eyes—not those eyes. Maybe because he'd lived in such a small circle, in such a tiny world, he'd never learn to harden his face as "normal" adolescents do. When I looked at him, his eyes were wide in what could have been delight. The nurse closed his eyes—she wore orange fingernail polish—and the doctor rubbed my arm. "We see many families here," he said, "but no family like yours," and then I cried. "You did the right thing," he said, but I had done nothing but follow Jamie's wishes. It was the hardest decision I'd ever carried out, but it would have been immoral and unethical to do otherwise—that much I finally understood.

Suddenly, my mother stood next to me. That she'd been dead for nearly a year seemed beside the point. "You did everything for this child," she said, pointing to Jamie, "now you go outside and make sure your other son doesn't walk in here unprepared." I nodded, and like the dutiful daughter I had been, I left the room. "My son died," I told the next-door sisters, who were standing in the corridor, looking stricken. I walked down the hall, to find the black nurse who had taken his blood. She met me halfway, put her arm around me, and walked me back to Jamie's room, where the sisters had a chair waiting. They gave me water, and like their biblical counterparts, sat at my feet and held the hands Jamie had left empty. His death was surprisingly like his birth: frantic, loud, and more of struggle than I ever would have imagined it to be.

Then I saw Patrick and Pat pushing through the door at the end of the hall. I stood up to meet them, putting my arms around them. Patrick Sr. was already crying, but Pat Jr. was flushed, and looked confused. "It's over," I said, and Patrick, now our only son, started screaming. *"What the fuck?"* he screamed *"What the fuck?"* and though his father and I tried to console him, he threw our arms aside, pushed past us, ran into Jamie's room, leaned over his bed, kissed his cheek, rubbed his hair. "Ah, no," he sobbed, "ah, no . . ." We took turns holding Jamie, so still, so white. This time it was Patrick Sr. who said he was sorry, sorry for it all.

Oh my God, Jamie.

When Father K. came back, he blessed Jamie, who'd turned bone white, like driftwood, or part of a Georgia O'Keeffe painting. "He's beautiful, isn't he?" Father K. whispered, and I sagged gratefully against him. There was so much of Father K. to lean on.

Good night, sweet prince, I said, finally, and then we had to leave.

We had to leave him, in that room, in his Knicks boxer shorts, and his Special Olympics sweatshirt, all Gatorade and Jell-O stained. We went down in the elevator, walked through the hospital lobby and through the front door, out into the spring sunshine—squinting, busted-up, a wobbly family of three once again, and into all the rest.

CHAPTER ONE

S HORTLY AFTER THE END OF THE CIVIL WAR, ALL BY herself, wearing her first pair of shoes, my nine-year-old great-grandmother Bridget Moore waved good-bye to her Mam, and her Da, and her nine brothers and sisters (including the never-named little brother who "walked funny," and fell down) and left Galway Bay for New York City, and a job as a Fifth Avenue "ladies' maid." Bridget brought to America a small steamer trunk, a pair of rosary beads, a clay pipe, and as near as we can figure out, Duchenne muscular dystrophy. In Ireland, she'd had little schooling. She'd never learned to add, or subtract, which was a bit of a hindrance when she'd finally saved enough to buy a Greenwich Village grocery store that she promptly lost when she couldn't figure out how much anybody owed her, and before it spoiled, simply gave her food away. Since Bridget had never learned to read, or write, she never knew what became of her family. She never heard from anyone in Galway Bay again.

But maybe Bridget Moore remembered her little brother

when her daughter Mamie's two sons, Harold and Raymond, and her daughter Sadie's two sons, William and Theodore, began "walking funny" and falling down. Maybe Bridget prayed for him, if she prayed for them, when she watched the sickness cutting through their legs like pinking shears through onionskin. Maybe Bridget finally mourned for her brother when she mourned for her grandsons, who were all under twelve years old when they died, of pneumonia, days apart, in February of 1922. In the front rooms of adjoining Hell's Kitchen tenements, at 403 West Fifty-sixth Street, an address that is now a parking garage, the four boys were laid out in two caskets. Perversely benevolent at the end, muscular dystrophy had whittled them small enough to lie in each other's arms.

While Bridget Moore was learning to live in New York, on the other side of the Atlantic, Dr. Guillaume Amand Duchenne, a French physician from a family of Marseille seafarers, was busy photographing the human face, or more specifically, the muscles of the human face, for which he received a prize. It was Dr. Duchenne who observed that genuine smiles not only use the muscles of the mouth, but also the muscles of the eyes—hence, the "Duchenne Smile." After Dr. Duchenne's young wife died in childbirth, he grew despondent, and left both medicine and Marseille. He resumed his career in Paris, where he became intrigued by a mysterious "wasting disorder" striking young boys, and opened a clinic. It was Dr. Duchenne who invented a "harpoon," an early form of muscle biopsy, to penetrate the skin of living subjects, and extract muscle tissue for examination. I can't imagine there were many "Duchenne smiles" after a procedure like that.

Dr. Duchenne's 1868 report, still in use today, lists fully the signs and symptoms of the "wasting disorder" affecting the legs, the arms, the hips of young males—all of the muscles *except* the muscles of the face. Enlarged calf muscles— ah, those enlarged calf muscles, melting into water and fat, where the dreams are first dashed—were the first symptom Dr. Duchenne noted. His patients died in adolescence, when their heart muscles, or their respiratory muscles, in the days before antibiotics, failed. Duchenne's discovery of the "dystrophy" that bears his name was not greeted with universal applause. "I thought humanity to be afflicted with enough evils already," one of Duchenne's colleagues pronounced, "I do not congratulate you, sir, upon the new gift you have made it."

In our family, it's the gift that keeps on giving.

Or, depending on how you look at it, taking.

After Mamie and Tom Timothy had buried Harold and Raymond, they were left with four other children: three daughters and a healthy son. But after Sadie and Jimmy Doyle had buried William and Theodore (James Jr., their first child, had died, in infancy, of spinal meningitis), they were left with only one child plucked from the wreck—a three-year-old girl, my mother Helen. Mom said that she didn't remember her brothers, or her cousins. She said that until she was about eight, and overheard her mother say something about "the boys," she hadn't known that she'd had any siblings at all, and then, Mom told me, their absence was what filled the railroad-style rooms. She was afraid to ask her mother and father about "the boys," her brothers, and so she asked Sadie's sister, her Aunt Nellie. "Your brothers' names were William and Theodore," Aunt Nellie said. "They had 'muscular apathy.' When they were only little boys, they stopped walking. They couldn't go to school. They were so weak that they had to be tied into kitchen chairs not to fall over. Then they died." And that was it. Mom said she'd wanted to know everything about William and Theodore. What they had looked like, how their voices had sounded, if they had "liked" her—even a little bit, but Aunt Nellie, who warned her not to be upsetting Sadie and Jimmy with her questions, no more questions, wouldn't say any more.

Then Mom said when she was about ten, while she was sitting on the stoop of the building, watching a neighbor's little girl learning to walk, the terrible thought struck her that *she* might have learned to walk while her brothers, tied to those kitchen chairs, were forced to watch *her*. She had to know, she said, and at the same time, was afraid to know, if her brothers had resented her.

But when Mom asked her cousin Evelyn, Mamie's daughter, twenty years Mom's senior, to tell her about "the boys," Evelyn had only laughed, and imitated how they'd hollered at her whenever Mom got into their things.

It wasn't until the 1950s that scientists realized that Duchenne muscular dystrophy (or DMD), like hemophilia, is a "sexlinked" disorder, carried by females and inherited by males. It wasn't until the 1960s, around the time that my brother Richie went into the wheelchair, that scientists discovered that female carriers of Duchenne muscular dystrophy (like afflicted males) had elevated blood levels of creatine phosphate kinase, or CPK, a muscle-burning enzyme. In those infantile days of genetic research, Mom, Pam, and I gave blood to the brand-new "genetics" department at Elmhurst General Hospital in Queens, New York. They found that although Pam and I had elevated CPK levels and were probably carriers, Mom's CPK level was normal—and she was not a carrier. "But Richie had DMD—how can that be?" we asked. They shrugged. They admitted that genetic testing had a long way to go. (Nearly forty years later, and detection of carriers is still only around 70 percent.) It would be years before they'd realize that at menopause, a carrier's CPK level often reverts to normal.

They didn't yet know that Duchenne is the most common and rapidly progressing dystrophy, or that the disease occurs in one out of every 4,000 male births. Even into the 1980s, figuring out which women were carriers, and which sons might be affected, was largely a guessing game. They knew that there was a 50 percent chance that daughters born to carrier mothers would be carriers themselves, and if they *were* carriers, a 50 percent chance that their sons would have DMD. They knew that despite the faulty X gene a female carrier inherits from her carrier mother, the healthy X gene she inherits from her father compensates. And unless there is a rare mutation, a female carrier will show no sign of DMD herself. If a son inherits his carrier mother's healthy X gene, he will be healthy, but if he inherits his carrier mother's faulty X gene, he will have DMD. A male gets only one Y and one X—there is no other X to compensate.

In the near future, the scientists said, a woman with cause to worry about DMD could find out, in the fifth month of pregnancy, if her fetus was male or female, and base her decision to "therapeutically" abort solely on the baby's gender.

For me, that would have meant aborting Patrick Jr., the deepest, most absolute joy of my life.

Like Mom, Pam and I are carriers. Duchenne muscular dystrophy is our heritage, our background, our pedigree. Harold and Raymond, William and Theodore, all died before their weakness became profound. Every skill my parents, Pam and Charlie, and Patrick and I had taught Richie, Jamie, Chris, and Jason, from brushing their teeth to combing their hair, to tying their shoes to cutting their food, and feeding themselves, DMD forced us to take back, until, in some terrible parody of parenthood, we were all bathing, dressing, carrying, feeding handsome bearded men in their twenties. You might have thought we'd have raised pedigree dogs, or blue-ribbon pumpkins, or even another kind of First Lady rose. The Ireland great-grand uncle, the Hell's Kitchen uncles and cousins, our brother Richie, my son Jamie, Pam's sons Chris and Jason, all the way from Woodrow Wilson through the second George Bush, we've been DMD's nieces, cousins, sisters, mothers, or some amalgam of them all. Always a bridesmaid, never a bride—although it sometimes seems about to get us too. Though there is no Paris clinic, or modern laboratory, where heartbreak and regret can be studied, they're wasting diseases too, eating though spirit and soul. (Even Sister Prejean, the death row activist, says that she can't imagine anything worse than seeing your child condemned to death through circumstances that are partially your fault.) Though we've had our moments, there weren't a lot of smiles, Duchenne or otherwise, in our hard lives.

If I could have, I would have slipped into one of those wheelchairs. I would have given any of the lost boys my healthy body. I feel as though I owed my brother Richie, my nephews Chris and Jason, my son Jamie, especially Jamie, that much. Richie had twenty-two years and Jamie had twenty-four. In Connecticut, in their increasingly more highly powered power chairs, now equipped with ventilator shelves, Chris and Jason, twenty-seven and twenty-six, are DMD geriatrics, struggling and enduring, day by day, indignity by indignity, breath by breath.

For over fifty years, I've had more than my share of movement. I've been walking on two good legs, moving two good arms, breathing, eating, swallowing without hesitation, without a single gasp, and all the while complaining about toothaches, headaches, head colds, paper cuts, bad hair days, free-floating ennui. Unlike the boys, I can turn over in bed, stalk out of a room, go for an angry walk, throw an innocent, blue-flowered Corningware bowl full of macaroni and cheese at Patrick Sr., who, though I don't remember why, certainly deserved it.

But DMD is a beastly thing, taking not only body and soul, but stepping on the throat of spontaneity, cleansing fits of pique, an awful lot of life's fun. In DMD, there are no young arms thrown carelessly around a shoulder, no pickup games in the school yard, no snowball fights, no diving boards, no

home runs, no touchdowns, no goals, baskets, girls, or weddings, no daddies, no babies smiling for the camera.

It was tempting to agree with the shrinks who thought they
were helping when they encouraged me to blame the Catholic
church for what was really our decision. "After all," so many of
them asked, "doesn't your church forbid birth control? Isn't it
the Pope himself who wants you to propagate and fill the
pews?" But the truth is that we were lukewarm Catholics and
the church was innocent. "Follow your heart," was what the
renegade Father O'Connor told us back in 1970, when
Patrick and I were about to be married, and asked about birth
control, and that was exactly what we did. Patrick Jr., all curls
and eyes, was the child of our hearts. When Pam and Charlie
looked at him, he was the child of their hearts too. Without any
rational reason to believe it, we were sure that DMD would
never happen to us.

When I was eighteen, just graduated from high school, I
worked for a rusty old bank in New York City's garment dis-
trict. Patrick was twenty, an electrical engineering major in
Manhattan College. We had very little money and so we
spent a lot of nights sitting on a bench in a small park on Sut-
ton Place, where he'd gone with his old girlfriend, the senator's
daughter. It was as though he'd never been on his way to the
seminary, where they told him he was too young and should
wait a year—long enough, as it turned out, for him to change
his mind—though he never completely abandoned the idea.
When we talked about getting married, he said he wanted
the Papal Blessing. When we spoke about having children, he

always said "if we should be blessed with children . . ." the both of us oblivious to the fact of Richie at home, in the wheelchair, watching *Combat* on TV. "Blessed with children," Patrick said, when everyone we knew was fussing with hair, burning draft cards, going nose to snout with the New York City mounted police. The nurses in the hospital thought Patrick was crazy when he insisted that our eight- and nine-pound, apparently healthy baby boys, be baptized right away—just in case. He said that parenthood was "a sacred trust" and I think *those* were the three little words that made me want to marry him, years before I'd wonder how "blessed" Jamie was with us.

It doesn't seem possible today that there was ever a time in my life when I hadn't heard the words *muscular dystrophy*. Though I couldn't yet read, and didn't know it had anything to do with our family, on one dog-eared page of an old medical book I'd found underneath my grandparents' bed was a picture I kept turning to again and again, a dozen boys wearing leg braces and sitting in wicker wheelchairs.

CHAPTER TWO

I WAS BORN IN 1950, IN QUEENS, NEW YORK. IN 1951, on the G.I. Bill, my parents bought a new house in Levittown, Long Island. By 1952, we were back in Queens. To say that my mother disliked suburbia would be like saying Hitler wasn't very nice. Until the end of her days, Mom referred to Levittown as that "gulag of flora and fauna." On the parkways, all of the moving vans were heading east. Ours was the only one heading west.

So rather than easing into the world wrapped in a warm blanket of sunshine and listening to sweet birdsong, in my first memory, I'm standing under the el, where it's dark and noisy and smells like bus exhaust. Nobody knows how near-sighted I am, that to me, the red and green traffic lights on Roosevelt Avenue look like fuzzy basketballs suspended in midair, and the Grey Nuns of the Sacred Heart whom Mom and I sometimes pass on their way back to the St. Joan of Arc convent, don't seem to have starched white cuffs at their wrists at all, but rather, thick white slices of mozzarella cheese. And when I look at the good sisters' feet, I don't see shoes but casters, like the ones on our hassock. On our way to the A&P, or Teddy's Meats, there are lots of people Mom and I meet, but unless they bend down, and look me full in the face, I don't know who they are. I can't see them.

Although I lived in a solitary, myopic world of hapless possibilities, asking my bewildered, high-strung, anxiety-prone mother if the good sisters chewed on their wrists when they were hungry, and did they take their wheels off when they went to bed, it wasn't what I couldn't see that bothered her. It was my pawing through the roof-dried laundry for the sunshine I told her was trapped inside, and my telling her that I could see Daddy's Aqua Velva crawling underneath my closed bedroom door that finally did it. Then she called Nana on the phone, and sobbed that I'd gone mental.

And then I learned to keep my fantastic world to myself.

Even when the statues in church winked at me, even when I heard the opera singer across the courtyard practicing her scales, and I watched the beautiful notes floating past the fire escape, more thrilling, to me, than any country birdsong—I kept it quiet. It was my first-grade teacher who told Mom that I needed glasses, and ruined everything. I might have stumbled over a lot of curbs, and had some nasty encounters with parking meters but I was happy in the soft, gauzy world I had, and not so happy with the sharp world my pink plastic harlequin glasses gave me. When I put on my glasses, and met the world for the second time, I was sorely disappointed. The statues at church weren't flesh but plaster, and the opera singer's "notes" were only incinerator ash. Everything was so much harder, homelier, grimier than I'd thought, and not nearly as much fun. Until, long before I started school, my mother sat me down, and taught me to read. Then, slowly, the world became a wonder once again.

I was the firstborn child, born when Mom was thirty-one, and Dad was twenty-nine, when most of their friends in the baby boomer, Eisenhower years, were onto their third and fourth. Like everyone else, they'd wanted a big family, but then Mom had two terrible miscarriages, the second of which had nearly killed her, and there was just me, being primed for an only child's pampered life. On warm, sunny days, Mom and I got into our mother/daughter dresses, our hats, our white cotton gloves, and rode the Q15 bus into the city. Schrafft's was where we had lunch, shrimp salad sandwiches, and "black-and-white" ice cream sodas and then we were off to Central Park, where we sat on one particular bench near the zoo, and my mother promised me a wedding at High Noon in St. Patrick's Cathedral, and then a horse-drawn carriage, and a reception at the Waldorf Astoria, or the Plaza—and almost as an afterthought, a doctor for a husband, Dr. Patrick Keats Yeats Parnell, so Irish his blood would run not red but green. On rainy winter days, on the brown living-room rug, Mom and I sat on a blanket and had a picnic of cream cheese and jelly sandwiches, and apple slices for dessert. With the flats of our hands, we squashed imaginary ants, until Mrs. Cunningham, the old bitch who lived underneath us, banged on her ceiling, our floor, with her broom. Then we laid on our backs staring at an imaginary sky. With her long auburn hair fanned around her head, Mom pointed out the Big Dipper and some of the other constellations, the ones she said we had clearly seen, though I didn't remember, from our Levittown back-yard. No matter how she'd swear she'd hated Long Island, any talk of Levittown made Mom seem sad. But then I climbed on top of her, belly to belly, my nose on hers, staring into her gray eyes, and she'd laugh. I could always make Mom laugh. Small return for what she did for me, filling my head with words, with stories, with memories I was never quite sure weren't mine, but hers. She gave me twice the life I would have had without her, and maybe that was why, later on, I gave so much of my young life to her.

Nana, Pops, and Aunt Nellie lived on the ground floor, in the building next to ours. Their apartment smelled of Oxydol, Ajax, Rinso Blue, all the old soaps, soft as confectioners' sugar be-tween the fingertips. On some days, the apartment also smelled of melted butter, vanilla, and cinnamon, and I knew the minute I opened the front door that Nana was at the stove, making rice pudding. It was always better to find Nana in the kitchen than Aunt Nellie, who didn't cook, but stood in front of the pantry with her arms folded over her formidable bosom in-stead, guarding the Mallomars on the top shelf. When I went to Nana, putting my arms around her slim waist, she said, "Hiya Chicken," her weird nickname for me, rubbing my shoulder with one hand, and stirring with the other. Her clean cotton dress smelled sweet, her bony hip felt sublime against my cheek.

When I think back on it, maybe it's important to fill a little kid's life with rice pudding, a clean cotton dress, a grandmother's bony hip, for who knows not only what will happen to them, but which moments will stick and one day, be the very thing that pulls them through.

In the early days, Daddy worked a lot of overtime, and Mom and I had our supper with Nana, Aunt Nellie, and Pops. After supper, wearing a starched white shirt (and sometimes, a bow tie) Pops sat in his red brocade wing chair, and I sat on the purple Oriental Woolworth's carpet, staring at his leather slippers, waiting for him to light his pipe, and tell me a story. I had my favorites. The day the lions escaped from the zoo, and terrorized the city. The family of twelve-fingered gypsies that lived in a tent by the river. As I got a little older, his stories got a little more serious. The young women he'd seen jumping from the Triangle Shirtwaist Factory to their deaths, the women and children he'd seen jumping from the burning General Slocum, the paddleboat that had left without Nana and Aunt Nellie, teenagers who'd cried because they'd missed the boat ride, and the picnic. Then there was his Hell's Kitchen neighbor, a Bromo Seltzer addict, who'd thrown the blue glass empties through Nana and Pops's open kitchen window. Pops told me that he'd spent night after night sitting in a chair by the window, catching the empties, and tossing them back.

Staring at me over the top of his tortoise-shell eyeglasses, through a cloud of sweet smoke, Pops said I should read Sherlock Holmes when I grew up. "Your Ma's a Doyle," he said, "and so are you. We're direct descendants of Sir Arthur Conan Doyle." (Well, maybe.)

Two decades later, on my grandfather's birthday, I met Mom's Cousin Evelyn in the butcher shop. Evelyn had softened with age, and I was a whole generation away from my mother, the little girl who'd gotten into her brothers' things. Evelyn told me that one day, right after the boys had died, she'd walked into my grandparents' kitchen unexpectedly, and came upon my grandfather, kneeling on the floor in front of my grandmother's chair with his head in her lap, and Nana stroking his red hair. She told me that it was Pops, a hotel steward, who'd brought whatever he could of the world home to the homebound boys, both his sons and his nephews. Cousin Evelyn said that the boys ate Charlotte russe, Hungarian goulash, and even pheasant under glass that Pops had said he'd stolen from Miss Lillian Russell's tray—or maybe it was Diamond Jim Brady's—he was never sure. He'd even told the boys that he'd walked in on Miss Sarah Bernhardt, who was not only naked but missing her wooden leg.

"It was Jimmy who'd buried the boys alone," Cousin Evelyn said, "when Sadie couldn't leave her bed. Your grandfather was a prince." With no idea of the gift she had just given me, Evelyn then took her ground round from the butcher's outstretched hand, turned and waved good-bye.

At seventy, Pops died in his sleep. It was the first great heartbreak of my life, but it was followed by the first great joy: Pamela Jane, with her mass of black hair. I don't know which was lovelier, or made me happier, the smell of Johnson's Baby Powder in my bedroom, or the words "baby sister." Two parents, two kids, a little more like everyone else.

Except that we had no aunts, no uncles, no first cousins coming through the door. On Thanksgiving and Christmas, and the odd days when Mom was sick with a stomach virus, Nana and Aunt Nellie were the only relations who came to our apartment. Wearing small hats, carrying big purses, their white faces set in grim determination, the old ladies hauled themselves up the four flights, staggered into the living room, and collapsed in the white leather Danish Moderne chairs to catch their breath.

On Sundays, Pam and I had no one to visit, and nobody came to see us. We stood on the sidewalk watching the parade of the other kids' cake-carrying kin pass us by. "How come we don't have company like everybody else?" I asked Mom. "It's just the way it is," she said. "I was an only child, and Dad's sister, your Aunt Shirley, lives in California. We *are* just like everybody else," Mom said, and that seemed true enough. Mom stayed home like the other mothers, going off with them to the movies on Tuesday nights, and like the other fathers, Dad took the subway to work, and played poker with them on Friday nights, dragging the card table from one apartment to the next. "It's just that we don't have a big family," Mom said, "not everybody does."

But one afternoon, when I was six, and staying with Nana, who was supposed to be "minding" me but instead, was fast asleep in the Morris chair, I wandered down the hall and into the kitchen where I got a chair, and dragged it to the coat closet where my grandmother kept her hatboxes. Trying not to breathe, terrified that the fox stole with the beady eyes on a hanger near the door was about to bite my elbow, I groped the shelf, and touched what I thought, at first, to be a piece of paper, but was instead, a picture of two children, a young boy with silky bangs and my mother's sad eyes, and a toddler with full cheeks and thick curls. When Nana coughed, I put the picture back, jumped down, closed the door, dragged the chair back into the kitchen.

"Those were my brothers," Mom said when I asked. *What brothers?* I wondered but my mother kept washing the dishes, and didn't say any more.

Then one day when we were with Nana and Aunt Nellie, Pam and I were holding hands, and dancing in their living room. The Philco was on, the screen covered in snow. We were watching—or trying to watch—what I now realize was an early Jerry Lewis Telethon. There were crippled boys in leg braces sitting in wheelchairs, on the stage, and Jerry Lewis was up-ending some woman's purse into her lap. Nana and Aunt Nellie laughed, but when Pam and I laughed, Aunt Nellie seemed angry with us. "Yiz girls are very lucky yiz can dance like that," she said, her shiny face flushed. I didn't know why she was so angry. I didn't understand what we had done. We were only playing, dancing in the living room, just as we'd done a hundred times before. "The boys couldn't dance," Aunt Nellie said, "they couldn't run, they couldn't even walk." She was either furious with us, or about to cry. I wasn't sure which. We didn't know anything about any "boys." Not knowing what else to do, I ignored her, and kept dancing with Pam, who was too young to know anything was wrong. I twirled Pam around the floor, my face burning with shame, trying to figure out what was the matter.

And then I thought about the picture I'd found, and somehow, I began to understand that those boys, and the crippled boys in the wheelchairs on TV, had something to do with each other. On *Superman,* I'd seen a crippled boy, riding on Superman's back. I thought it looked like fun to be crippled. Everyone Superman and the boy met were so nice to them. I pretended to be crippled myself, pretending to limp, dragging my left leg along the sidewalk to see if anyone would be nice to me, but the only one who noticed was my mother, who shook my shoulder and told me to knock it off. Then she brought the both of us to Buster Brown shoes not for the U.S. Keds that all the other kids wore but for brown leather oxfords that laced tightly across the instep. Summer and winter, we wore "good sturdy support shoes," as heavy on *our* legs as leather braces.

Pam was small, agile, and seemed to adjust quickly to the ugly oxfords, but I was bigger, slower, and I found it hard to run. Those shoes made me aware of every step, every skip, every jump from one apartment house stair to the next. With every game of jump rope, hopscotch, tag, I thought about the crippled boys, the mysterious crippled brothers who couldn't run, or couldn't walk. Walking and running had become my obsessions. For the first time, in a more certain way, I was aware of being different, a "different" that had something to do with my legs. We didn't know it yet, but our days of passing for "normal" were almost over.

CHAPTER THREE

RICHARD CARSON KEHL, JR., MY BROTHER, WAS born in May of 1957, when I was seven and Pam was nearly four. Mothers and their newborns stayed in the hospital about a week in those days, and twice a day, Dad, who'd taken a week of his vacation, drove back and forth to see them. Too young to go to the hospital, Pam and I spent that very long week with Nana and Aunt Nellie, who bickered so much that they gave us headaches, and told us that our whinging was giving them "the pip," an animal disorder, I would later learn, that was strictly limited to chickens. It made sense. After all, Nana called the both of us "Chicken"—what else could we give her but the pip?

Pam and I patiently endured Nana and Aunt Nellie's testy, old-lady attempts to care for us, eating more creamed food than we'd ever seen in our lives, closing our eyes at the raw eggs stuck to the bottom of the bottomless glasses of chocolate milk. When Nana and Aunt Nellie sat us in the bathtub, and handed us wash rags, we earnestly tried to figure out not only what, but where exactly, our "kitty murphys" were. They called our blouses our "waists," and were forever asking us if we had to "cock a potty," which we finally figured out when they gestured frantically at the toilet, meant "go to the bathroom." Without Mom there to translate, we were lost. Not only was there a secret language at Nana and Aunt Nellie's apartment, but they saved everything my mother threw out. Used aluminum foil, old Christmas cards still in their envelopes, skeleton keys that fit none of the apartment's locks, and wads of dirty string. They saved everything, even their old fights.

"What's the matter with your hair?" Sister Mary Anthony demanded to know on the day that Aunt Nellie had sent me to school with my hair, under my pink glasses, completely covering my right eye—like Veronica Lake, the "famous movie star" Aunt Nellie knew about, but I had never heard of. When I came into Sister Mary Anthony's classroom, I stumbled over a desk. But no matter how terrible *my* hair looked, I knew I'd gotten off easy. I'd left Pam sitting in the couch, looking traumatized, staring straight ahead. Nana had made Pam's ponytail so tight her lips were pale, and flat, and she looked Chinese.

On the day that Mom and our new brother were to come home from the hospital, Dad let me stay home from school. Pam and I were too excited to eat, too excited to sleep, too excited, practically, to sit still. We got up at dawn, dressed ourselves in our orange big 'n' little sister Easter dresses, and sat on the sofa to wait. And wait. And wait. More than Christmas, more than Easter, we yearned to see this new brother, the mysterious Richard. I thought he'd be blond-haired and handsome, like Timmy on *Lassie,* have baseball cards, be able to ride a two-wheeler, and even tell me dirty jokes like the boys in my class.

But when Nana's front door finally opened, there was no brother that I could see, only Mom looking pale and thin, and Dad with an armful of white blankets. It was only when Dad knelt in front of us, and pulled the white blankets back, that I realized our new baby brother was *in* the blankets. It was pretty clear, even to me, that our new brother didn't have baseball cards, couldn't ride a two-wheeler, and since he didn't even seem able to talk, didn't know any dirty jokes. He was small, round, red, bald, and ugly. He didn't look like Timmy on *Lassie* at all—if anything, he looked more like Fred Mertz on *I Love Lucy.* When he squirmed in his blankets, and began to wail, so did I. In his lacy bassinet, he looked more like a pointy-headed apple than a brother.

That afternoon, despite Mom's protests—"I don't feel up to it, Richard, I look a mess!"—Daddy bought cold cuts, and packed Nana and Aunt Nellie's sink with beer and ice, and invited everyone we knew to the apartment. After two girls, he finally had his son, no small thing to a father who'd wanted a Marine. We'd never seen Daddy so happy, dancing with Nana in the bedroom doorway despite her protests—"My arthritis Richard! I haven't danced in years!"—sweeping her into the living room, past the big buffet table filled with ham, potato salad, creamed herring, salmon cakes. He held Pam's hand, and my hand, and he twirled us around the floor, our stiff crinoline slips brushing against our thighs. The neighbors came, and the distant cousins came, and Dad's friends from the barroom came too, and everyone got along. It was amazing to see how nice Mom could be to Dad's barroom friends when she wanted to—although they were a little leery of *her* since the Christmas Eve she'd found Dad in the Rendezvous, playing shuffleboard, and she'd upended the shuffleboard table onto the floor. There was all that beer in the sink, and Mom didn't seem to notice how much of it Daddy drank. She thanked our company for the presents they brought, smiled at them, shook their hands, let their tentative kisses brush her cheeks. It amazed me that a brother as ugly as ours had made everyone so happy, when, only a week before, things had been so different.

After Dad came out of the bedroom where he'd been talking to the doctor on the phone, his face flushed, his eyes glistening, and told us that the new baby was a boy, Nana had jumped up from the Morris chair, burst into tears, and ran down the hallway into the kitchen. *"Jaysus, Jaysus,"* she cried. It was so quiet that when she ran past us, we could hear Pops's gold wedding band clicking against hers on her long, skinny finger.

Dad looked at us, we looked at him, Nana sobbed in the kitchen.

"Nana's very old," I whispered to Dad, "sometimes she says crazy stuff." Though I never saw a single cowboy, or horse, she was always telling me she was "heading for the last round-up." Sometimes she said she had cancer of the mouth, and she wouldn't stop showing us her tongue.

But Daddy, who accepted everyone and everything, no questions asked, took it in stride. "What is, is," he liked to say, and so when Nana ran by, he didn't spend a lot of time looking after her. He shrugged, and opened the big brown bottle of beer that was waiting on the coffee table for the three of us, a "special treat" Dad had called it, a big glass for him, and two tiny glasses for us that he'd filled right after the doctor called. It hadn't seemed like much of a special treat to me. It was much too bitter. As bitter as Mom became whenever she saw a bottle of the stuff standing on the kitchen table. Usually she grabbed it, and dumped it in the sink. We drank it anyway, raising our glasses, drinking and shuddering, and staring at Daddy, toasting our brand-new baby brother.

And then, before we knew it, Daddy was standing in Nana's living room with the baby in his arms, turning his slim hip so that the men in the room could see the cigars, like brown pencils, sticking out of the back pocket of his chinos. "My future Marine," Daddy said, showing Richard's face to almost all the men he knew, the former soldiers and sailors who'd been at Normandy, Iwo Jima, the Philippines—unlike Dad, who'd wanted to make the Army Air Corps his career but was sent home at the height of the war to support his eighty-year-old grandmother and his orphaned teenaged sister. "Hear, hear!" someone shouted, and then everybody clapped, and somebody stomped his feet, and somebody else whistled so loudly that my ears hurt. They kept saying that our new brother was a "beautiful little boy" but I thought everyone was crazy. He didn't look that good to me.

After the company left, Pam and I were sent to sleep in the "high bed" in Nana's room. When I woke up, and saw that the baby's bassinet was at the foot of our bed, I jumped down to look at him. Though he was asleep, I reached in and picked him up the way I had seen my father do, but when I did it, something was very wrong. The baby's head sagged, fell back, and he started to scream. Terrified, I put the baby down, and burst into tears myself. (In twenty years, my brother's neck muscles would be so weak that when I pushed him in his wheelchair, his head would fall back in exactly that same way, and I would feel that terror all over again.) My father burst through the bedroom door, his white undershirt bluish in the pitch dark. He bent over and grabbed my elbows. "I broke the baby," I cried. "No," he said, "no," taking my hand, and leading me to the bassinet. "Like this," he said, slowly picking the baby up, carefully supporting his head. He carried Richie to the flowered chair by the window, the streetlight outside filtering through the shade, and sat down. By this time, Pam was awake and leaning against me. "Put your arms out," Daddy said to me, and when I did, he placed Richie into them. "All you really need to do is support his head," Daddy said, and although I'd been prepared for the worst—my mother could be brought to blood-curdling shrieks by a spilled glass of milk—that was the end of it.

How I wish I could go back to that moment and somehow change all the years that followed. I'll never stop wondering if Richie had been the son Daddy had wanted, if Daddy would have been the father we needed. Pam and I got back into bed, and I fell asleep watching Daddy sitting in the flowered chair, staring at the tiny son in his arms.

Then it was summer, the baby never stopped crying, and the lights were always on in the hot apartment right under the roof. Mom never seemed to sleep. She was up all night, walking the parquet floors, with the screaming baby in her arms.

Early one evening, Dad came home from work to find the potatoes boiling on the stove, the three of us stretched out on the sisal summer carpet, and Mom sound asleep in the living room chair. He picked her up and carried her, fully dressed, including her shoes, and put her on the bed.

One hot day when Mom had the three of us washed and dressed and sitting under the big tree in front of the apartment house, waiting for something—anything—to happen, a blue Bel Air convertible pulled up, and a smiling, pimply faced man got out. "Jimmy!" Mom said, standing up. "Hi Helen," he smiled, and before we knew it, Mom was climbing into his car, and Nana and Aunt Nellie were at the kitchen window. "Jaysus! Jaysus!" Nana shrieked as the Bel Air pulled away from the curb, "Yer Ma's gone off with her old beaux, that eejit Jimmy Courtney! She's gone and left yez!" Even at seven years old, I knew that Mom would never leave us. Half an hour later, Mom was back, standing in Nana's kitchen, pulling Richie out of Nana's arms.

"For Christ's sake, Mother," Mom said, "I only went for a little ride in his new car. It was the only way I could get rid of him!"

Although Nana would eventually forget most everything— her own name, Mom's name, her sister's name, our names, and even had herself convinced she had misplaced her rectum somewhere at the 1964 World's Fair, she never forgot the day Mom "abandoned" her family, and ran away with "that eejit, Jimmy Courtney."

CHAPTER FOUR

IME PASSED, RICHIE LOOKED BETTER, LESS RED, more pink. His grayish eyes turned an amber brown, and white blond hair sprouted on top of his head. He looked like a strawberry cupcake with coconut frosting and smelled like the vanilla in Nana's rice pudding. At every baby sound Richie made, Pam and I ran to the bassinet, but we could've just as easily walked. The apartment was so tiny we were never more than a few feet away from one another. My father used to say that our apartment was so small that he could shave with his right hand in the bathroom, and make coffee, in the kitchen, with his left.

Everything about our cupcake baby brother was delicious, from the soft folds in his neck to his wrinkly fingers and toes. Pam and I could hardly keep our hands off of him. When Mom wasn't looking, we crept into our parents' bedroom, reached into the bassinet by Mom's side of the bed, and held his hands, or pretended to bite his toes. Or we stood behind his head, and made silly noises just so he'd turn and look for us. When he tried to turn over, in his diaper and T-shirt, the back of his neck looked so tender and soft I could barely stand it. I had to turn away. He was just so small. Though sometimes he hated it, it was fun to press our noses to his, and stare into his dark eyes—until he cried, and shook his head as if he were trying to wake from a nightmare. Then Pam and I were in trouble, and Mom sent the both of us down the twelve-inch hallway, and into our bedroom. Pam's was an old iron bed that some ancient Irish relative had expired in, and mine was a maple bed with an expensive "horsehair" mattress that my parents had splurged on when they thought I'd be their only child. We sat on our beds, across the room from each other, and our knees touched.

When he grew too big for the bassinet, Richie was moved into our room, and slept in a peach-colored crib that had been a stubborn, virulent pink when it belonged to a neighbor's little girl, resisting all of Dad's careful efforts to paint it white. The white crib that Pam and I had slept in was long gone. Nearly forty when Richie was born, Mom never expected to have any more children. She told everyone that he had been a "surprise," though I didn't understand what she meant. Her belly had been big for such a long time—how could the baby have been a surprise? It seemed as though we'd been waiting all our lives for him. When he was in our room, Pam and I crept into his crib, nuzzling his neck, rubbing our heads into his belly. We loved to make him laugh. Every morning, it was like a present to sit up in our beds, and see him sitting quietly in his peach-colored crib just waiting for us. It amazed me that the ugly, Fred Mertz baby he had been was now so pretty with big bright cheeks, and eyebrows and eyelashes so thick they seemed to be made of felt, like Mr. Potato Head's. Coming down the four flights on our way to school, Pam and I laughed at how silly he'd looked, sitting in his high chair in his yellow footie pajamas with pablum cereal smashed all over his face. He was just waking from his morning nap on Mom's bed, when we came home for lunch, and then we laughed hysterically at the chenille tracks in his pink cheeks. At dinnertime, he sat in his high chair, his sticking-out ears bright red from the cold, when he was supposed to be feeding himself, but fumbled with his silly white spoon instead, and dropped most of his dinner on the floor. Once, when she was clearing the table, Mom showed me the spinach cross that had formed on Richie's plate. "A blessing in disguise," she said, but I didn't know what she meant. I didn't notice anything "in disguise." We were up to our eyeballs in blessings then, and Richie was just one more.

But Richie didn't walk until he was fourteen months old, and when he "ran," it didn't look like running at all, but hopping. Richie hopped. First on one foot, and then on the other. He had trouble climbing the stairs. Clinging to the bannister, Richie pulled himself from one step to the next.

Mom said that Richie was just "immature," that some kids are just a little slower than others. "A lot of kids have trouble with the stairs," Mom said—although I couldn't think of any. All of the kids on the street, even little ones like Richie, were climbing the stairs two at a time.

"A lot of kids take a while to learn to run," Mom said, "you never ran fast either," she said to me, and it was true. Pam was much faster. And we could see for ourselves that Richie was very short, and for him, the stairs were very high. Mom said that Richie would learn to climb the stairs in time, and he would learn to run, but as time passed, he didn't get any better at these things. If anything, he got worse.

When Mom thought we were asleep, she tiptoed into our bedroom and leaned over Richie in his youth bed, and rubbed his calves. Though she never realized I was watching her, she rubbed his calves when he was lying on his belly on the brown rug watching cartoons and she rubbed his calves while he was sitting on the sofa next to her, playing with his toy soldiers. Whenever Richie sat next to Mom, she rubbed his calves and whenever Pam or I sat next to her, she rubbed our calves too, holding our legs this way and that, pressing her index finger into our flesh. All she knew of the muscular dystrophy that had killed her brothers and her cousins was that it started with big calves. (Although a boy with DMD appears to have the muscular legs of an athlete, the truth is that his calf muscles are falling apart, and are being replaced with water and fat. The legs that give a DMD boy such trouble on the sidewalk are lighter than air in a swimming pool.)

But Mom didn't remember the boys and she didn't know what else to look for.

Later on, Mom would talk about one particular "moment of knowing," when Richie, then only a few months old, was sitting on her lap in the front seat of our aqua-and-white Ford, and his legs felt, as she described it, "peculiar." By that time, Pam and I'd had our own "moments of knowing"—Pam, in a Missouri Air Force Base, when the pediatrician spent a long time looking at Christopher's eight-month-old legs, and me, at a birthday party in Queens, when a father elbowed me, pointed at Jamie's legs, and said, "He's gonna be some bruiser!" and it was as if an icy metal cleaver neatly sliced my life in two. By then my sister and I knew exactly what Mom had meant.

My grandmother, who knew exactly what muscular dystrophy looked like, who couldn't even bear to look at the only picture of two of her three lost sons, never said a word about Richie's troubles. And despite her fears, Mom never mentioned his "immaturity" to the pediatrician. The doctor never said a word about his legs, never asked him to climb stairs, run, or even get up from the floor, something that was getting harder and harder for him to do. Richie was never sick, Mom told us, and his checkups were fine. Why look for trouble? Even we could see that Richie was a happy little boy with a gentle temperament who laughed a lot and ate everything in sight. He was funny, and he was smart. Even Dad, who didn't have a lot to say and was rarely ever home, said that Richie was so bright, we should call him "Sunny."

And "Sunny's" two-step, running/hopping didn't seem to bother him much. Richie's own attempts to run seemed to strike him as ridiculous anyway. When he saw us watching him try to run, he rolled his eyes, and made us laugh. But then, he began to fall. He fell on the sidewalk. He fell in the bathroom. He fell in the kitchen, and in the living room, right on top of his plastic soldiers spread all over the rug. Then he stopped rolling his eyes, and we stopped laughing. We told him it wasn't his fault. We blamed the uneven pavement, the wet spots near the tub, the glossy linoleum by the door, the toys under his feet, the lumpy spots on the rug. In the winter, we told ourselves and anyone who would listen, that Richie fell down so much because of his bulky gray snowsuit and in the summertime, we blamed the heat, or maybe he needed glasses, or his sinuses made him dizzy, desperate for reasons, hurtling through space, losing the idea of the "normal family" we'd been what seemed like only moments before. What had happened to us? What was wrong with Richie? What would happen next? Mom, Pam, and I were forever picking Richie up from the sidewalk, steadying him on his feet, dragging him up the four flights of stairs. We had to protect him from eager dogs, unsteady toddlers, from the crew-cut boys whizzing through the streets on skinny English racer bicycles with baseball cards clothespinned to the spokes, from the curious eyes of the neighbors, who, like us, couldn't understand, in the Thunderbird days of the late 1950s, a little boy who had such trouble moving about in the world.

"He has a little trouble with the stairs," Mom, Pam, and I said to the mailman, and the Con Ed man, and the super trying to pass by. My mother watched her son struggle with the stairs, and my grandmother watched him struggle with the stairs, and Aunt Nellie too, and they looked at it and wouldn't see it, and hoped, I imagine, that it would all just go away. My father was the only one who couldn't stand to watch, and when Dad was around, he carried Richie up and down, and anywhere he wanted to go. Like Richie, Pam and I couldn't understand what was happening. We were as bewildered as he was. At dinnertime, when it was time to go home, and she had to start dinner, my mother went upstairs ahead of us, leaving Pam and me to get Richie home. Pushing him up the stairs from underneath his small backside was slow and tedious work. It was quicker to pick him up by the belt loops of his pants, one stair, steady him, and then the next, and if that didn't work, then I just carried him, and Pam carried his coat, though Mom didn't want me to do that. She was afraid that we'd all fall. I could barely stand hearing his groans, his colossal effort, and then how exhausted he seemed, eyes shut, pink face pressed against the bannister.

"He has a little trouble with the stairs," we whispered to cranky old Mrs. O'Brien, who seemed anxious to pass, but instead, stood glaring at us from the bottom of the staircase. "What're ye mumblin'?" she demanded, but we were too ashamed to answer her, too ashamed to look up and see our trouble-making selves reflected in her black, raisin-like eyes. It was a Mt. Everest climb for us, and we couldn't look any of the neighbors, who thought we were playing and were angry at the inconvenience, full in the face—and so we stared at their shoes, feet passing by us so effortlessly on Mercury-like wings. Mrs. O'Brien, in her black orthopedic shoes, Mrs. Cunningham, the old bitch who lived beneath us, in her cut-up carpet slippers, with the bunion that looked like a parsnip—even the slender Meenahan bride, impatiently tapping her delicate pink Capezio, her signal for us to move aside and let her pass, the Geir's Meats bag dripping blood behind her. Softly, quietly, we cheered for Richie when he managed one step, and then the next one, huffing and puffing worse than Nana with her arthritis, and worse than Aunt Nellie with her "bum hip," and they were in their seventies, and he wasn't yet four. Pam and I had homework to do, cartoons to watch. We were hungry and sometimes *we* got angry at him. "You're so *slow!*" we hissed, "come *on,* Rich!"—but both of us had to look away, for his dark eyes, the eyes I still see in my dreams, were trying so hard. Every step pulled Richie farther and farther away from the beautiful baby he had been, and the family we thought we were, and the blessings we thought were ours.

In the days and weeks and months that followed, Richie fell so often that scabs were mixed in with the freckles on his nose, and he often looked as if he had the measles. His chin was black and blue. He had purple lumps on his forehead, new scabs or the old ones ripped open on his knees. Those poor knees, shredded too many times to count. Mom followed him with icebags, face clothes, iodine, Band-Aids. Boys will be boys, people said, and despite her early moment of knowing, it was her moment of denial, for Mom agreed. One injury after another. That's what happens when you have a son. Meanwhile, Richie hit his face so often that he lost his baby teeth before they were wobbly. Even his knuckles were rubbed raw from the sidewalk. We couldn't understand why he didn't put his arms out to break his fall, not knowing that he had already lost that response. It was amazing that he never broke any bones, or needed stitches. Someone was always around to stand him up, dust him off, pretend that things were fine, for as weak as he was, he was somewhat flexible, and many of his falls were not abrupt but more like a gradual sinking as his legs gave way. He was frightened, staring at us from the pavement. When we got him to his feet, he banged his fists against his thighs, calling for the kids on the street to wait up. Sometimes, when they were waiting for Richie, not looking where they were going, the kids smashed into things—trees, the streetlights, each other—and then they fell down. At this, someone else on the sidewalk for a change, Richie roared with laughter—but then he fell. He fell if he laughed too hard, if he had too much fun, if other little boys pulled off his hat, if the little girls tried to grab his hand, and pull him along. They were just kids, like Richie, like us, and there was nothing Pam or I could do but leave the jump rope and hop-scotch and stand near Mom, in case one of the kids fright-ened Richie, made a funny face, patted him too hard on the back, and down he'd go. "Go and play with the kids," Mom said, "I'll take care of Richie," but we couldn't do it. It was too hard. When Richie was on the sidewalk, games didn't matter. Nothing but Richie not falling down mattered. I couldn't wait for Richie to grow up, get older, be better, and until then, I wanted to be there in case he fell.

Kruschev was at the U.N., banging his shoe on the table, and threatening to bury us all, and I was sitting under my desk at St. Joan of Arc School with my head between my knees at an air raid drill, listening to the timid kids cry. I didn't care about Khrushchev, or his bombs. I just wanted my brother to run, climb stairs, race up and down the street like Pam, like me, like everyone else in the world. Why not Richie? What was wrong? Like Guipetto with Pinocchio, all I wanted was for Richie to be a real boy. I just had to find some way to help him.

CHAPTER FIVE

I N ST. JOAN OF ARC SCHOOL, THE GREY NUNS OF the Sacred Heart said that faith could do amazing things. I tried to have faith that Dad would stay out of the bars, and stop drinking beer, and faith that Mom would stop being angry with him all the time for being in the bars, and drinking beer. I thought that if I had enough faith that Jesus would perform a miracle for me, too, like the one at Cana, but this time, change all the beer in Heaney's into water, but that didn't work out at all. I figured I didn't have enough faith for that, and told myself I needed a lot more. I wanted to be like St. Christina the Astonishing, whose faith led her to rise from her coffin and soar to the rafters to escape the stench of human flesh, or like St. Perpetua, whose faith led her to guide a Roman soldier's sword to her throat. But I didn't quite understand what faith had to do with any of this. Why did "faith" demand that St. Rose of Lima rub pepper into her pretty cheeks, and lime into her beautiful hands? On matters of faith, my mother was no help at all. "Faith, schmaith," my mother said, rinsing out the bathtub, "it's all a load of crap." "What about faith moving mountains?" I challenged her. "Well, okay," Mom agreed. "Faith can move mountains. And if your aunt had testicles, she'd be your uncle." ("Why did you send us all to Catholic school?" I asked my then seventy-five-year-old mother, who'd consistently thrown the *Brooklyn Tablet,* with its movie ratings, into the garbage and instead, let us go and see whatever movie we wanted, and at Christmastime, rolled her eyes at the Happy Birthday Baby Jesus birthday cakes in Shelley's Bakery window. "It was closer than the public," she said.)

It was clear to me that faith couldn't do a thing for fathers and beer. To me, all that fussing with mountains was a big waste of faith. In pictures in my geography book, the mountains looked fine exactly where they were. Wouldn't moving them leave tremendous holes, and after we moved them, where would we put them? I was going to have extraordinary faith that God would fix my brother and turn him into a normal boy. And so I kept my First Communion Rosary beads in the pocket of my school uniform, and my corduroy pants, and my flannel pajamas, and for Richie, obsessively prayed my way through the decades. City kids had so much more freedom then, and when I was supposed to be at Girl Scouts, or the library, or off on errands for my mother, or even looking in the front window of Heaney's for my father, I snuck into church, said a Hail Mary, and lit a candle for Richie. Whenever we neighborhood girls, wearing our mothers' pinched silk scarves, lying on the ammonia-scented tiled lobby floor, played nuns (while the neighborhood boys were over in the school yard, shooting hoops), it was for my brother that I prayed. I wanted to have more faith than St. Christina, St. Perpetua,

St. Rose of Lima. I didn't think I was asking for a lot from a God who'd created the earth, cured the paralytic, gave sight to the sightless, raised Lazarus from the dead. Didn't He know that fixing Richie would be a cinch?

We needed a miracle, but even living in an apartment building with an elevator would have helped. Why didn't we move? Perhaps because we knew everyone on the street, perhaps because Nana and Aunt Nellie were right next door, perhaps because moving was expensive, and our rent was cheap, though nothing seems enough reason to struggle the way we did, from the world at the bottom of those four flights of stairs, to our life at the top. Moving seemed such an exotic adventure. Other than the young couples still fleeing for the suburbs ("Forgive them Father," Mom said, for they know not what they do.") few families on our streets moved. Instead, we put our name on the super's list for the next available ground-floor apartment, but by the time we got one, it was 1966, and Richie was in a wheelchair.

In the meantime, I couldn't understand why my prayers weren't working, why Richie wasn't getting better, but worse. Maybe praying just wasn't enough. There were a lot of kids at Mass on Sunday mornings, and Richie was so small. Maybe God wasn't noticing him. Maybe God was distracted by the kids wanting new bikes, Betsey Wetsey dolls, or a home run for the Yankees, all those silly prayers buzzing in His ear. I thought that God might notice Richie more on a Saturday morning, when there were no other children in church. If only God would see how easily he fell, how hard it was for us to pull him up the church steps, how delicately I had to guide him to the pew—maybe that would work. I knew I'd notice Richie more on a Saturday morning, a little kid in the middle of all those old ladies with their ragged novena booklets, and their long strings of amber Rosary beads.

"I guess," Mom said, one Saturday morning, when I asked if I could take Richie to church. She was so unsuspecting, vacuuming the carpet, dusting the windowsills. I wondered what she'd say when Richie became a normal boy and she found out that I was the one who'd gotten God to pay attention.

On Saturday mornings, through the long winter of 1961, I buttoned Richie's navy blue jacket, tied his red woolen hat underneath his chin, slipped his red "mitties" into his pockets, and we set off for Mass. I was eleven and he was four, making the slow and careful journey along the quiet streets. He was starting to have trouble at the curbs, and at the start of every street, I had to pull him up onto the sidewalk. I pretended not to notice how hard walking was becoming for him, and so I kept talking as we walked, pointing to the red-and-white cartons of pigs' feet and tripe in the window of the butcher's, the dusty palm trees and silver plastic airplanes in the window of the travel agency, gingerly and carefully raising his arm so we could both wave at the tiny people planted on the tiny decks of toy cruise ships.

In the window of the grocery store, I pointed to the cans stacked in the window, their labels so faded from the sun that the contents were illegible. Richie couldn't read yet, and so I invented the stuff inside. Canned rabbit, creamed alley cat, mouse stew. I had to hold his hand tightly in case he laughed, for then he'd fall down. In the windows, I stared at our reflections. We looked so normal when we stood side by side, like any little brother and older sister.

When we got to church, we sat in the front pew where God couldn't miss us, but Richie wasn't interested in the Mass. Seven years old might be the church's "age of reason," but Richie was only four. I hoped he wasn't undoing all the prayers I was saying. "If we are in God's house," he asked, "then where is God? Where does God sleep? Where is God's bathroom?"

"Where is God's TV? Does God watch cartoons?"

Please God, help him, I prayed, staring at Richie as I hoped God was too. *Help him,* I prayed, *help him,* until it all ran together. *Helphimhelphimhelphim,* and when I did that, I felt for the moment, that I had done all I could possibly do. Patience is a virtue, the nuns said, right up there with faith. All I had to do was wait and see.

After Mass, Richie was tired, and it was harder to keep him on his feet. I scanned the sidewalk in front of us for anything he might slip or slide on, or trip over. All that looking down sometimes had its advantages—sometimes we found loose change. Those were the lucky Saturdays, when we stopped at Don's for candy or gum. Richie took forever to decide. "Kids," I sometimes said to Don, eleven years old and as phonily exasperated as any mother in a peanut-butter commercial. Don laughed, with me, or at me, I never knew, and I laughed too. Week after week after week and Richie didn't get better. Week after week after week and God didn't seem to be listening.

By the summer of 1961, Richie cried a lot. He didn't always eat his dinner, and he didn't care who had the last raspberry metropolitan cupcake in the green-and-white Larsen's box. When the kids on the street made fun of him, walking on their toes like he did, with their bellies sticking out, Pam belted them with the wiffle ball bat that Santa Claus had brought Richie, but that Richie could never use. Then Dad got involved. Though it was a Friday night, Mom didn't have to send me looking for Dad. He was home early, sitting on the sofa with a big bag in his lap. He took out an inflatable Bazooka Joe punching bag, the bottom weighted with sand, and a pair of boxing gloves. Dad tied the boxing gloves onto Richie's hands but when Richie swung, he lost his footing, fell, and hit his head on the coffee table, Dad picked him up, sat him in the chair, left the apartment and went up to the roof. Mom ran after him, and then a few minutes later, so did I. I stood in the shadows, and stared at their backs. My father's white shirt and my mother's green skirt, both billowing in the wind, made my parents look like frightened little kids, in clothes much too big for them.

But when I came back down to our apartment, the boxing gloves on the table gave me an idea. Everybody knew that Richie's legs were weak, but what if we could prove that his arms were strong? After all, he pulled himself up from the floor, and from one step to another, didn't he? What if Richie were to box Bernie Clark, a boy his age who lived down the street?

"I don't know," Pam whispered in our dark bedroom, while Richie, oblivious, in his youth bed by the door, slept on. I had to make her see what I did—Bernie Clark, a head taller than Richie, sitting on the sidewalk stunned, and Richie smiling. Pam and I holding his hands in the boxing gloves over his head, like the *Daily News* pictures of Sugar Ray, the Champ!

"It'll be easy," I told Pam. She would just get Richie's boxing gloves while Mom was hanging clothes on the roof, and come downstairs to where the kids were gathered on the sidewalk, with the gloves hidden underneath her shirt. "We'll meet Dad at the corner, on his way home from work," I pleaded, "and we'll tell him that Richie won. 'No kidding!' he'll say, and then he'll whistle . . ."

"I don't know," Pam said again, but I finally had her convinced, and before we knew it, we were tying gloves onto the little boys' hands.

But all Bernie Clark had to do was jump in front of Richie like a real prize fighter, with the gloves close to his nose. Richie was so scared he fell down. He crumpled to the pavement and hit his head, and instantly, his blond crew cut glistened with blood. Someone got Mom, running down the street with her hair in curlers, her hands smelling of disinfectant. "What's wrong with you?" Mom asked me, her blue eyes watery, for I was the oldest. "Don't you know any better?"

And I didn't. "Told ya," Pam said, and she was only eight.

We kept trying.

While Dad worked overtime, and Mom washed the dinner dishes, Pam and I tied our jump rope from the leg of the coffee table to the leg of the end table. "Jump!" we whispered, Pam taking Richie's legs, and me, holding him underneath his arms. We jumped a little, until Mrs. Cunningham began banging on her ceiling with the broom.

And then it was time for Richie to go to school at St. Joan's, and though I don't know what my parents were thinking, that Richie was just immature, that he'd suddenly be better, as immersed in magical adult thinking as I was in my childish thoughts. Richie was registered for first grade just like Bernie

Clark and a lot of other kids. There were stairs in school, stairs in church for the mandatory 9 A.M. Children's Mass, stairs everywhere we looked, and Richie less and less able to manage them. Like the other older siblings in the neighborhood, Pam and I were expected to take him back and forth to church, to school. Not to do so would be too suspicious, and as a result, and we were always rushing, always late, always terrified.

"What 'trouble with the stairs'?" the Grey Nuns who saw me standing at the bottom of the huge marble staircase in back of the church after the Children's Mass, demanded to know. Mom and Dad, waiting for us at home, went to Mass together later—Dad in his good navy blue suit, and Mom in her beige silk dress, the both of them doused in the cologne of denial. Because I was older, my grade sat in the back of the church, and our class was the first one dismissed. I waited for Richie at the bottom of the stairs, and when the other grades began filing out, searched for him in the crowd. When I finally spotted him, I could hardly restrain myself from running up the stairs and grabbing him, so ready to catch him should he fall that I could barely keep my arms at my sides.

In memory, he wears a red Eton blazer, white shirt, red-and-blue polka-dot tie, and a red cap that the other boys are forever snatching and tossing among themselves. Navy blue, wool "short pants," the great globelike muscles of his tiny, thick legs like oranges pressing against his navy blue knee socks. There had to be long pants in Richie's young life, wintertime, corduroy, heavy wool, but I don't remember them. His legs just wouldn't let me look away.

"If your brother is old enough to be in school," the Grey

Nuns said, "he's old enough to tend to himself," but they didn't see what I did. So many shoving, pushing kids on that top step, grabbing for one another's collars, jumping on each other's shoulders, and Richie in their midst, bright-eyed, laughing—and so perilously close to disaster.

"Wait outside," the Grey Nuns said, although all I was trying to do was catch Richie's eye as if I were an air traffic controller, and could bring him down safely. The Grey Nuns wouldn't listen, didn't understand, grabbed the collar of my camel-hair coat and pushed me out onto the street to wait for the dreadful screams or the terrible thud that amazingly, incredibly never materialized.

That Richie was never seriously hurt was the wrong miracle perhaps, but a miracle nonetheless.

CHAPTER SIX

THREE SHEETS TO THE WIND ONE HOT FRIDAY night in 1965, after another day of installing telephones in the WPIX building in New York City, Dad came off the subway wearing a giant-size pair of Kelly green fur feet props he had pinched from the set of actor Chuck McCann's kiddie show. In those days, he was always taking home weird things—an entire bottle of soy sauce from the New Cathay Restaurant underneath the el, a huge bundle of paper towels, Lucky, our black puppy, and a thick pen that stood on end, and revealed a naked lady (never mind the stairs, and the falling—when Richie brought that pen to St. Joan of Arc's first grade, it was a whole other story), but the green fur feet were the first weird things he'd taken and actually *worn*.

On that Friday night, he was so late that Mom, Pam, and Richie and I, once again, were sure he was dead. I imagined the four of us following his casket down the main aisle of St. Joan of Arc Church. Wondering what I'd wear to Dad's funeral made me feel very guilty. Mom put Richie on my back, and once again, the three of us headed for the subway, only it was summer, and we had an entourage: Pam's friend Patty, one of the O'Rourke boys, Mom's friend Dolores. We all stood at the foot of the subway stairs, and waited. Suddenly we saw the green fur feet coming down at us, the long curved claws, like grotesque fingernails, gripping each step. At first we were relieved, then we three wanted to kill him, and then—surprise—Mom laughed. To see her laugh at him rather than scream at him was a gift. People passing by looked down at Dad's green fur feet, smiled, and shook their heads. On that hot night in Jackson Heights, for just a little while, though Dad was full of beer, and Richie couldn't walk, we were a happy family. Sort of. Not happy in any way that Tolstoy would recognize, just happy for us. Because Mom had laughed at Dad, and Dad had laughed too, it was okay for us to think of him as eccentric and we could think of the green Chuck McCann feet as another of Dad's fashion faux pas that Mom blamed on his succession of motorcycle-induced fractured skulls, adding to the gray shirt covered in red forks and the pink swimming trunks covered in red cabbage roses that were Uncle Bud's California cast-offs.

If only he could have stayed sober. God, we might have laughed a lot.

Dad came not only from a long line of drinkers, but a long line of drinkers who were, sometimes down to the skin, inappropriately dressed. His father, Harold, a World War I hero, the son of Bible-thumping Dutch Reformed Protestants, went through the Depression years with a snake tattooed on one arm, an eagle on the other, and a naked woman ("September

Morn") on his chest. There was Dad's bigamist Uncle Tom, who bought not only cars but white, ten-gallon hats with checks he'd forged from one of the rich widows he'd married, until he was unceremoniously carted off to Sing Sing. Then there was Dad's Aunt Minnie, known to take a nip or two, buried wearing her glasses, and a homemade cotton print dress with a big red bow in her hair. This was further proof to my teetotaling mother, as if she needed it, that my father—and his family—weren't operating on the same channel as everyone else. Not only was my mother's Irish family sober, but the men didn't wear ten-gallon hats, had been married only once, hadn't been to Sing Sing, didn't have tattoos. They came from completely different backgrounds. While my grandfather Jimmy was taking my mother to Bickford's for pancakes on Sunday mornings, my grandfather Harold was teaching my four-year-old father to swim by tossing him, fully dressed, into the deep end of a swimming pool.

The men in my mother's family had navy blue suits for the weddings, and the wakes, including their own. But when the women in my mother's extended family died, it was very different. Their wakes, at Walter B. Cooke's Funeral Home on Roosevelt Avenue, were a kind of "opening night," when the ladies went off to the hereafter in elegant gowns, beautifully coiffed and made up, like Irish Gabors.

When my mother came home from Aunt Minnie's wake, she was clearly disappointed. She told us that Aunt Minnie had looked as if she were waiting for the bus. My grandmother, who'd been minding us, staring at the clock the entire time with her big black purse on her lap, sniffed. "What did you expect?" she asked my mother, "from that black Protestant blood?"

No matter what color his blood, my father had left clues that he was a little different than the Declans and Swithins my mother had been dating most of her single life. The night they'd met, my mother had been wearing a flowered rayon dress like the other young women at the party, but my father, unlike the men, wasn't wearing a wool suit. He'd just gotten off his Harley and not only was carrying a crash helmet underneath his arm, but was dressed head-to-toe in black leather. My mother, who'd spent her life surrounded by fair-haired, light-skinned Irishmen was instantly smitten. Dad was "drop-dead gorgeous," Mom always said, the best looking man (outside of Clark Gable) that she had ever seen. She said that when they'd met, she'd been "a twenty-nine-year-old virgin" (thanks for sharing), still sleeping on the living-room couch, who went to her secretarial job at Continental Can every day with a lunch her father had made for her. Cream cheese and jelly on pumpernickel bread, tongue with mustard and butter—sandwiches that didn't travel well, but to Mom's coworkers—imagine! a father who makes your lunch—were nevertheless endearing.

Young and energetic when she met Dad, Mom worked hard to get him off the Harley and into a Rambler, out of the leather and into gabardine, out of the crash helmet and into a fedora, away from the bad crowd and into a regular life. In the beginning at least, truth be told, Dad did his part. He sold the motorcycle, and though Mom was at best a halfhearted

Catholic, he became a convert. He tried to be what my mother wanted, though late in her life, Mom said she wished she could go back, and stop her younger self from wasting so much precious time and energy trying to change Dad into someone he was not. She said she could have cured cancer with the effort she had squandered. Sometimes, she said she should have married Elmer Teller, her first serious boyfriend, Irish or not. Never mind about her married name being "Helen Teller"—it was only a name after all, and Elmer Teller didn't drink. She said that Dad should have had that Army Air Corps career he'd so badly wanted, though she couldn't understand it at the time—during the war, everyone she knew wanted to get *out* of the service, and Dad was the only man she'd met who'd wanted to stay *in*. But he was an orphan with an elderly, widowed grandmother and an orphaned teenage sister to support, and he was nothing if not responsible. Off the motorcycle, out from underneath the leather, away from the drink, he'd had so much potential.

With how it turned out, I think that my father should have stayed on the motorcycle, and spent his life in the barroom company of the world's unfettered, tattooed Trixies, Jockos, and Slims. I think he might have been happier. While my mother the fiancée was bringing to her marriage her grandmother's trunk filled with the silk peignoirs Aunt Nellie had stolen from Best & Company, and Aunt Julia's hand-embroidered linens, my father the fiancé was bringing to his marriage a cedar closet filled with fishing poles and hunting rifles. To placate my mother, Dad didn't get rid of the guns after I was born, but instead, as a safety precaution, took the handle off the cedar closet door. Until I was older, I never knew what was inside the cedar closet and neither did my grandmother, for when our parents were out and Nana was minding us, she spent most of her time in my parents' bedroom, digging at the door of the cedar closet with a butter knife. But if Nana never quite trusted Dad, it was his own fault. Staring straight into her eyes, a crazed expression on his face, wiggling his ears, lying though his teeth, Dad had told Nana that the fractured skull scar on the back of his head was where "spacemen" had implanted a steel plate, that "they" sent messages to his brain, that they wanted him to take them to his leader, and Dad said he was going to bring them directly to Mom.

If he couldn't be an outdoorsman in the middle of Queens, then Dad had wanted to be a policeman, or a fireman, and though he'd scored high on the tests, my mother begged him to walk away—and for her, he did. She wanted him to be safe. Mom was overjoyed when Dad went to work in the city, as a installer for the telephone company. She loved the city—the city, she said, was where she was "bred and buttered." "Think of the excitement!" she said, "so much to see and do! And the city is the safest place in the world . . ." she added, as if she weren't talking to a country boy who liked to hunt, and fish, and was rolling his eyes at her. He didn't give a damn about safety. He knew—though my mother yet didn't—that the danger he was in was all on the inside. No matter how hard she tried, my mother couldn't save him. No matter how many birthday presents, anniversary presents, Christmas presents, cards upon cards, notes upon notes, no matter how many times she plopped into his lap, or how many after-dinner hugs and kisses she encouraged Pam and me to give him, crawling all over him, trying hard to burrow into his sweet-smelling, roof-dried T-shirt, and his strong slim back while he lay so perfectly motionless on the couch watching *Gunsmoke* that he let us slip to the floor. Even before Richie was born, Dad couldn't, or wouldn't, be repaired.

Though we didn't know what was wrong with Daddy, we all thought—especially Mom—that with enough work, he would surely change.

And so on Friday nights before Richie was born, Mom, Pam, and I got all dressed up and rode the subway into the city to meet Dad after work, waiting for him in one art deco lobby after another, taking a taxi to the automat for dinner (where my mother would invariably forget to put a cup underneath the coffee spout until it was too late) and then, afterward, a long walk together along Fifth Avenue. But it was always more complicated than that. The minute the elevator doors opened, and my father, in his workingman's clothes, a fat ring of building keys hanging from his belt, stepped out and saw the three of us standing there, he often started to cry.

It was not only perplexing for us, but embarrassing to see stragglers walking through the lobbies turning back to stare at him. Standing underneath those harsh lights, across that expanse of cold marble floors, he seemed so alone that we could barely stand it, and in a flurry of Sunday coats, freshly curled hair, pocketbooks, and shiny shoes skidding on the slippery marble, we charged at him, desperate to stop any more tears from running down his angular face. Pam and I hugged him, Mom hugged him, kissed his cheek, and with her glove, dried his tears. Pam and I grabbed his hands, smiled up at him, made our eager jokes. He was so different than he was at home, rubbing our heads, wrapping his arms around our shoulders, hugging us close to his side. It didn't stay, but in those lobbies, for small bits of time we savored and relived, Mom had the husband she worked so hard for, and Pam and I had the Daddy we longed for and loved.

Everyone said it was my brother's muscular dystrophy that killed Dad long before the drink ever did, and they might have been right. In 1979, when Richie died, it was his boyhood friend Marine Sergeant Patrick O'Rourke walking into Walter B. Cooke's Funeral Home in dress blacks that literally brought my father to his knees. Though we didn't understand it at the time, there was a hole inside my father that couldn't be filled. Not with devotion, not with understanding, not with love, not with two little girls, and a wife eager to try. Not even, I suspect, with a strapping son who became a Marine. Generation after generation, if there is one lesson to be learned above so many others, it is this: No one can save anyone else.

"Man takes a drink," my poor mother said to my poor father, on sober Sunday mornings, after the latest humiliation, wagging a finger in his face, "and then the drink takes the man."

When my father was the one taking the drink, he was also taking crazy old Uncle Willie, Nana and Aunt Nellie's ancient, morose brother, for his weekly shock treatments, and afterward, when Uncle Willie was wrung out like a rag, carried the old man into Nana's back bedroom, and put him to bed. When Dad was the one taking the drink, he was fixing the neighbors' broken washing machines, or taking them down to the curb, to save someone's back, or someone's heart, or carrying the new ones up again, saving someone else the delivery. With a tiny moustache brush, he dyed not only my mother's hair, but some of the neighbors' hair too, and he made a small cardboard sign for our kitchen's pockmarked wall: Salon Ricardo. On the morning of my tenth birthday, when my mother sent him to the record store for some Neil Sedaka, or Elvis Presley 45s for my new "hi-fi," he came home with Tommy Dorsey, and Glenn Miller—yet it didn't matter. All the little girls at my birthday party waited in line to dance with him, and he twirled each and every one, their crinolines flashing from underneath their party dresses, all around the living-room floor.

When he was the one taking the drink, he let all the neighborhood kids pile on my parents' bed while he read "Dr. Seuss" to us in "Reginald Von Gleason's" snooty voice. On Thanksgiving Day, when Nana became suddenly convinced that she couldn't walk outside the confines of her apartment, my father put her on his back, and carried her up the four flights. When he was the one taking the drink, he was also making three or four summertime trips from our broiling street to Kissena Park, and back again, so that none of the neighbors would be left out of a Sunday picnic. And we brought along Dad's "super-duper" homemade swing—a sanded and painted "seat" Dad had cut from a wooden board he'd bought at the lumber yard, and tied to a sturdy tree with a length of heavy rope.

When he was the one taking the drink, Dad brought me fishing, and taught me to bait a hook, and gave me a fishing pole of my own (somewhere along the line, he'd emptied the closet, and finally sold the guns) and brought me—just me—

fishing at the Rockaway docks. My mother was imaginative, high strung, talkative. Like her father before her, stories upon stories fell from my mother's lips, and broke over my head like waves. They were as important to me as the very air I breathed, but it was in the silence of my father that I recovered. My mother was quick to anger, easily provoked, liked to argue, but my father waved it all away. Needing so often to be forgiven, he forgave everybody everything.

When my father was the one taking the drink, I could lean against him, my shoulder pressed against his arm, my thigh next to his, and though I still couldn't burrow into him, we were outdoors together, looking out onto the water, and I understood what it was to be at peace with another human being.

Then the drink took him, picked him up, threw him into thundering rages he never seemed to remember, fumbling all over himself with apologies for our bruised arms, and the occasional black eye that we blamed on the falling ironing board. "Yer da's a rummy," was what Nana said, looking at our arms and weeping. "He doesn't mean it," was what Mom told us, and when Dad was sober, showing him the bruises on our arms, legs, or faces, although it was risky. Sometimes, the bruises he inflicted were what set him off again. We were always so eager to forget about everything and start anew.

There were days when he'd seemed scared, in flannel pajamas, lying on the sofa when we came home from school, claiming to have a cold that none of us could see, doing the newspaper crossword, watching the game shows, trying desperately, it seems to me now, to hang onto his sanity while my mother, grateful to take care of him, eager—as if she could— to fix what was wrong, brought him endless bowls of soup and countless cups of tea on a big silver tray—but the drink took him anyway, day by day, beer by beer. The sad yet funny father we'd loved was being swallowed up inside that other roaring beast, and there was nothing we could do but watch.

And yet, when it came time to take Richie to the pediatric neurologist, Mom, the sober one, the one we could all depend on, the hub of our family wheel, collapsed in the recliner chair, and couldn't move. Though it seemed to take everything he had, and might have well been what finally pushed him over the edge, when Richie needed a diagnosis, it was Dad—trembling, fragile, sober, who stepped up to the plate.

CHAPTER SEVEN

E XCEPT FOR THE KIDS, ALL OF MOM'S SECOND AND third cousins were going to Cousin Grace's fancy New York City wedding—even Nana, who hadn't been out of the house since V-J Day. An actual Kennedy sister, Grace's college friend, was going to be there, and Mom could hardly wait. Usually a last-minute shopper, Mom had her navy blue silk dress and matching peau du soie shoes in the closet for months, right next to Dad's new Robert Hall suit. The day before the wedding, all that Mom had to do was run over to Mr. Shine's Millinery, and buy a navy blue hat. The last thing she expected to do was go blind.

To hear Mom tell it, she very calmly finished washing the bathroom floor. She said she knew her sight would come back. No, she hadn't been scared at all. She knew exactly what had happened. Her nervous system had gone berserk.

But I remember it differently.

I remember a tearful, terrified, panicky Mom, running out of the bathroom, banging into the closet door, groping the end tables, the coffee table, the top of the TV searching for her keys. I remember how smudged her lipstick looked when she locked the door, and how, for the whole four flights, she tapped the end of each stair with her toe, and that she was wearing mismatched shoes. I didn't dare tell her that she was carrying two different purses. I'd learned from past experience that Mom had degrees of "berserk"—the day she went blind, she was really cooking.

She dumped Pam and me in Nana's kitchen, and then ran across the street to Dr. Placek's office. As we looked through the window and watched Mom coming back, it was clear that Dr. Placek hadn't been able to fix whatever was wrong. She looked crazy crossing the street, groping the rounded fender of a Rambler sedan and then making a zig-zagging break for it.

When Mom got to Nana's apartment, she threw her head down on Nana's kitchen table and sobbed. She said that she was still blind, and Dr. Placek had been no help at all. He'd said that she had something that sounded like "miner's asteria," but she wasn't sure, for after all, when she was nervous, her hearing went too. Why, he'd even had the audacity to laugh when she'd asked about a cure! She said that was when she'd gotten up, grabbed her purses, and stomped out of his examining room.

"Has anyone here ever gone blind?" she said she'd called out to whomever might have been in the waiting room, sitting on those uncomfortable leather couches, for she didn't need to see or hear anyone to know they were there. There were old people in Dr. Placek's office nearly every day, Mom said. They were a million and two years old, for Christ's sake, and there wasn't one disease they hadn't had, or hadn't heard of—but nobody answered her.

"But maybe they did . . ." I said, and she heard me clearly enough to send me into Aunt Nellie's bedroom, where there was nothing to do but stare at the hula doll Aunt Nellie kept on her windowsill.

I heard Mom tell Nana that she should have stopped smoking, but she didn't, and now she had some miner's disease, probably something like the black lung she'd read all about in *Life* magazine—only in her case, it had attacked her eyes, and it was so terrible that no wonder Dr. Placek had laughed when she'd asked about a cure!

"Jaysus, no!" Nana cried, jumping up from the chair with her hand clamped over her own mouth. Then Nana called Dad at work, and told him to call the doctor, for Mom was very, very sick, there were children to raise and he couldn't be depending on her, for she was headed for the last roundup.

Dad was a man of few words, and when he called back, he asked Nana to put Mom on the phone. He had two words for her, and a little advice. "Minor hysteria," and she should toss a canary into her mouth.

"Oh," Mom said, pulling her head up from the red oilcloth and hanging up on him.

Only because Mom was blind did Nana agree to come along with us to buy Mom's new hat, only Nana wasn't much help. Pam, who was four, had to hold Nana's hand, for Nana was so busy looking for Japanese planes that she wasn't looking where she was going and kept tripping over the curbs. I held

Mom's hand, for I was seven, and Mom was much more trouble than Nana. At least Nana stumbled quietly. Mom cursed when she tripped not only over the curbs, but over small dogs, kids on skates, and shopping carts. *"Son of a bitch! Bastard out of hell!"* Or every now and then, *"Sacred Heart Protect Us!"* She didn't see all those people who were sitting on the half wall in front of the post office staring at us. Then the hat that Nana picked out, plopped on Mom's head, and paid for turned out to be black, and not navy blue at all. When Mom could see again, there was hell to pay. To Mom, the possibility of an actual Kennedy sister seeing her in a blue dress and a black hat was so intolerable that she and Nana had a big screaming fight and stopped speaking to each other. Until they got to the Hotel Pierre for the reception, and found themselves seated side by side at a dark table behind the kitchen door. *The nerve.*

When Mom's nervous system went berserk, she couldn't swallow, and she couldn't hear, and she couldn't see, and her bowels turned fickle. She grew absentminded and lost things— so many tickets that the dry cleaner wouldn't give her anymore, so many wallets that she took to carrying the table money in an old Con Ed envelope instead. The only trouble was that she mailed her table money so many times that they got to know her at the post office. They thought she was working undercover.

Dad never said that Mom's nervous system had gone berserk. He simply said "your mother is in her throes," and usually, he was the one who'd put her there. Wallets, dry cleaning tickets, Con Ed envelopes Mom could replace. When Mom lost Dad somewhere between wherever he was supposed to be and the Liffey Tavern, she was not only "in her throes," but out of her mind. Three hours late for one Thanksgiving dinner, full of apologies and Fleischman's whiskey, Dad was standing in the kitchen doorway when Mom hurled the turkey at him. Leaking buttery onions and Bell's Seasoning, it skidded along the linoleum floor until he stopped it with his foot, and then we ate Franco American spaghetti, mashed potatoes, and cranberry sauce—which the "experts" were convinced caused cancer.

The last time that Mom was in her throes, or her nervous system had gone berserk, was on a hot day in August of 1965, when eight-year-old Richie finally had an appointment in New York City with the pediatric neurologist who was supposedly "the best in the business." That morning, not only couldn't Mom get out of the living-room chair, but she couldn't take her nightgown off, or pull the curlers out of her hair. She couldn't stand up long enough to wash her face. In a year, she'd be spending lots of time on the phone with other mothers, and even the grandmothers of handicapped kids she'd meet in hospital clinics throughout the city where she'd take Richie for one thing or another. For awhile there, it was as if they could fix him piecemeal with occupational therapists, physical therapists, orthopedists, neurologists. Mom would talk research, treatment, cure, and not only for muscular dystrophy, but for cerebral palsy, and retardation, for deformities of all types and kinds. Strangers would cry on her shoulder, strangers would kiss her good-bye. In depressing and dismal surroundings, Mom was the one who'd compliment a broken child's new outfit, pretty smile, bright eyes. She was the one who'd tuck a stuffed animal into a child's artificial hand, and never so much as flinch. Dad could only see what was, but Mom, who sprinkled hope like fairy dust, could always see how things might turn out. "Where's your faith?" she'd ask me at rough spots in Jamie's MD journey—but I couldn't always answer her. I could never keep track of it. From one minute to the next, I never knew where my faith would be. I must have lost and found it a million times over. My mother believed that sick kids can be cured, that hereditary diseases aren't always passed on, that this time tomorrow, you'll be standing inside a new day. She had the gift of the blarney, a child's innocent heart, and could never stand for anyone to lose hope. She blamed herself, and suffered quietly watching three of her four grandsons in wheelchairs.

In one of the sporadic journals she kept in the mid-1980s, she wrote:

> I can't put my hands on their head and cure them. Forgive me, dear daughters, for what I so innocently caused. The wonder is that you don't blame me—but you don't have to. I blame myself. I curse my blood every day that I live. I curse my ancestry for all of it.

On that hot day in August of 1965, it was Dad who got Richie up and dressed, gave him breakfast, helped him brush his teeth. From the kitchen window, I watched them get into our "whitey Ford," and pull away. Richie stood in the back—

no seat belts in those days—with his head resting on Dad's shoulder. In their crew cuts, they looked so much alike. And then they were back, and Daddy, wearing sunglasses with tears streaming down his cheeks, was standing in our bedroom doorway.

"It's muscular dystrophy," he said, barely able to get the words out, "and we're going to treat Richie very nicely from now on." Years later, he would tell us that when the pediatric neurologist diagnosed Richie, he also suggested that Daddy join the Muscular Dystrophy Association and "ring doorbells" before offering Daddy a roll of coins as his "contribution." Choked up, anguished, I nodded. We adored Richie. Weren't we very nice to him already?

By the time I came out of the bedroom, the recliner chair was empty and Mom was dressed, made up, and standing in the kitchen where, despite the heat, the pots were boiling, and it was business as usual. My mother, usually so gifted with words, had left it to my father to tell us what was wrong. We went outside to where Richie and the O'Rourke boys were sitting in front of the apartment house where the steps were covered with new toys my father had bought—G.I. Joe dolls, a footlocker, a tank, and a jeep. Ah, those lovely O'Rourke brothers, with the sparks in their soft blue eyes, their tender brogues. "Why is everyone being so nice to me?" Richie wanted to know, but we didn't know what to say. Pam picked up his toys, and I carried him, and we brought him inside our apartment, to our familiar steaming kitchen, but an unfamiliar life.

Then it was September, and every day, by subway, I was on my way to Cathedral High School on Lexington Avenue in New York City. I'd become obsessed with legs again, not allowing myself to think what else Duchenne muscular dystrophy would take from my brother. For now, the legs were enough. What made one pair of legs stronger than another, I'd wonder, looking up from my James Michener paperbacks to the actual legs across the aisle, and in front of me, and the legs leaping from subway car to subway platform, and back again. I couldn't stop staring at the pictures of legs in miniskirt ads and shoe ads and ads for Virginia Slims.

It amazed me that people moved so effortlessly, so thoughtlessly, on their legs. No matter how the train lurched, people stayed so nicely balanced, with their strong legs spread wide apart. The faces around me might have been grimy and worn, but the legs—the legs were the miracles. "Dancer's legs," they said of Richie, before they knew why his calves were so big. I was fifteen, no longer a child, yet I was certain that God would suddenly realize His mistake and take it all back. Richie's home run would be the one to win the World Series, and I would tell all the reporters that we'd thought he'd had muscular dystrophy when he was young, and it would be so preposterous, we'd have to laugh.

In the meantime, when it was too hard for Richie to walk back and forth to school, Dad put the training wheels back on Pam's blue bike, and four times a day, Mom pulled him back and forth, and carried him up and down the stairs. Slim to begin with, her weight plummeted to little over a hundred pounds.

In the reference books at the library, I read every word I

could find about muscular dystrophy. Some of the books said "retardation" was a symptom, but that was so wrong, it was almost funny. Richie was smart and funny. When I read that most boys with muscular dystrophy were dead by the time they were twelve, I closed the book, left it on a table, and ran home to my mother, who was in the house almost all the time, cooking, cleaning, doing laundry, and when he was home, taking care—more and more and more care—of Richie. I was only a teenager, and there was so little I could do to help: all that I had to give my mother were my words. In my mind, I photographed everything that I looked at, from the set of an old lady's mouth to a child's tantrum in Woolworth's, mulled it over, made it funnier or more poignant than it really was, made it mean more somehow, kneading the outside world as if I were shaping bread for the pan, waiting for it to rise, and baking enough for two. Fancy foods were what my grandfather brought home to the lost boys, but embellished words were all I had for Mom. And it worked. Mom told me that the minute I came through that door, everything in her life seemed alright—that I was the one thing she could count on to make her forget my father's drinking, my brother in the wheelchair.

CHAPTER EIGHT

N A BRILLIANT OCTOBER DAY IN 1966, IN THE BED-room the three of us shared, while Mom, Pam, and I cheered him on, Richie took his final steps. He was nine years old. I can still see his freckles, his fading summer tan, his tongue poked out of the side of his mouth as he concentrates on getting from the bed on one side of the room to the bed on the other. He stepped through a sunbeam on the wooden parquet floor—Emily Dickenson's "slant of light"—and that was it. It was time for a child's wheelchair, an visual oxymoron if ever there was one, so hard on the eyes. My brother had finished walking forever.

I watched Richie, Jamie, Christopher, and Jason all take their last steps, and I know that right around the time of the wheelchair, DMD boys appear to be at their healthiest, as if DMD has put down the gun, and is possibly reconsidering. To look at a DMD boy in his very-early adolescence, with shoulders just starting to widen, and hands starting to spread, it seems entirely possible that the whole thing is just a character-building episode in what will no doubt be a long and healthy life. To his parents, a nine-year-old DMD boy is a sweet preview of the adult he still might become, like a movie trailer with one wonderful scene. It's almost a surprise when DMD awakens with a blood-curdling roar, and tears at the meaty shoulders, the sturdy trunk, the thick, childish neck—and leaves that valiant, optimistic, misdirected Adam's apple. The strong emerging nose turns bony, the bright eyes sink, and there is a sad, gaunt face whittled from the round-cheeked boy of only a moment ago. There's no way to get through it without covering yourself in something like what would one day—and a few presidents later—be called a "Star Wars" shield. Smack dab in the middle of the sixties, on the last day that Richie walked, there were all those Age of Aquarius possibilities in the very air we breathed, and DMD's days seemed numbered. We really believed that Richie would survive.

"Dance, Richie!" Pam cried, twelve years old and not ready, not then, not now, to surrender. She jumped up from the bed, and grabbed Richie's hands, but he couldn't do it, and clung to the bedspread instead. Pam burst into tears, ran into the bathroom, and slammed the door. Stunned, Richie looked at Mom and me. "Oh, Pam doesn't mean it," my mother said, but she wasn't very convincing.

Trading Pam's blue Schwin bike for the brown Everest and Jennings wheelchair changed everything. Though he didn't yet look it, Richie was handicapped, crippled, unwell—there it was for all the world to see. There was nothing more to hide. You can't argue with a wheelchair. "Wanna make something of it?" Pam asked the neighborhood kids in an encouraging voice while holding a persuasive wiffle ball bat over their heads, but nobody took her up on the offer. When Richie went into the wheelchair, it was a huge, almost giddy relief, especially when Mom assured us that he would someday get *out*. There's a lot of research going on, she told us, it's only a matter of time. There was no more worry about stairs, sidewalks, curbs, rain, snow, ice, toddlers, old people with canes, dogs, scooters, slick magazine pages. Although it seemed like someone's idea of a sick joke that Pam and I were such big girls when our brother was so tiny, we were strong enough to push him anywhere, through anything, or take him out of the wheelchair and carry him anywhere. To the balcony of the movie theater, to see the Ice Capades at Shea Stadium, way up in the cheap seats, for there was no handicapped seating in those days. We went for long walks, to toy stores, for ice cream sodas, chocolate milkshakes, for pizza, and we dragged all the neighborhood kids, sparks glowing all over the place, who proved not to need the wiffle bat but instead, fought over who would push the wheelchair when Richie could no longer do it himself. We laughed a lot on our excursions, Richie most of all. Laughing didn't knock him down anymore, and he had a lot of laughing to make up for. There was nothing sweeter on a Saturday morning than looking out the kitchen window and seeing one of the O'Rourke boys riding on the back of Richie's wheelchair, with his arms wrapped around Richie's still-strong neck. I could almost feel the wind in Richie's hair.

It was such a paradox—when Richie was "confined" to the wheelchair, he had more freedom than he'd ever had before.

If anyone asked what was wrong with him, Mom told us not to lie. "He has muscular dystrophy," she told us to say, replacing the old "he has a little trouble with the stairs."

"But don't forget to say that we have a lot of hope," Mom said, for she was Irish, and nothing is more insulting to an Irishman than even a drop of pity. Kindhearted, dopey people sometimes asked if Richie couldn't get in to see that Dr. Salk— although all that polio and muscular dystrophy have in common is a wheelchair. Some who were neither dopey nor kindhearted asked Pam and me, defenseless in our miniskirts, if our children would have DMD too, as if it were something we'd aspire to, a showcase for our goodness; and those were the people we didn't know how to answer, for we were Mom's Irish daughters and surely bred to be polite. Mom told us to smile sweetly, and say that DMD would soon be a thing of the past. Because, after all, that was true. That was a good sturdy answer that we used a lot, and each time we did, we believed it a little more. "Oh, it'll never happen to your kids," Mom said, although we hadn't asked, as if she were reading our minds, and that was what we told ourselves. We were just like everybody else after all. She wanted it so much to be true, and we wanted it to be true and all that wanting made it feel like a certainty. It hadn't happened to any of Cousin Grace's boys. (Lucky Cousin Grace, whose mother, Cousin Evelyn, had hidden from her daughter the whole DMD family saga.)

"And even if it *does* happen," Mom would sometimes say, while Pam and I grew uncomfortable, "there will surely be a cure by then. Look at how good Richie looks!" and we looked at him, and it was true. His legs could no longer support him, his arms were growing weaker all the time, and yet he looked, if no longer wonderful, at least normal, still able to "pass" and he seemed happy in spite of it all. "It's the age of miracles!"

Mom said, "We have to have faith. And if Richie doesn't have a chance at being cured, then nobody does."

Nearly forty years later, and nobody gets out of DMD alive.

But Mom didn't mention the mornings when Richie looked terrible, and seemed miserable. When Mom was carrying him from the toilet to his bed to dress him, he was often downright teary. On those mornings, she balanced him on the side of his bed, and knelt in front of him. She held his face in her hands and looked into his eyes. "Richie," she said, "listen to me. Someday, you'll get out of this wheelchair, and you'll walk again."

When Richie was upset, Dad not only stayed away from the bedroom but out of the house while Pam and I stayed behind, pretending to poke in the closet for a sweater, or a pair of shoes, and listened. We needed to hear every word. (This was long before we laughed that not only would Richie be cured, but Daddy would stop drinking and we would win the lottery.)

The Good Sisters wanted Richie to stay in St. Joan of Arc School but there were stairs, and fire drills, with only the wobbly-legged janitor to carry him up and down. Richie went off to public school, which in those unenlightened times, meant that all ages and disabilities were lumped together in one classroom. Then Mom kept him home, fought the New York City Board of Education, was threatened with arrest, until Richie, along with a few of his classmates whose parents joined my mother's fight, was enrolled in Human Resources School in Albertson, Long Island, where he wore bell-bottoms, tie-dyes, a striped headband, and though his fingers were curling in on themselves by then, made peace signs. His favorite subject was English. My mother remembered her shorthand, and Richie dictated his assignments. Whether his compositions were about robins, the culture of Peru, or his summer vacation, they all began the same way:

"When I get out of this stupid wheelchair . . ."

At the end of the day, Richie rolled through the door and said, "Home is the best," and Mom grinned. She was determined to make home the best, trudging five blocks to get our meats from the Kosher butcher, who gave us not only healthy chickens but their surprised-looking feet sticking out of the bag. She bought new slipcovers, new drapes, new end tables that she kept shiny with lemon oil. The kitchen floor and the bathtub were always clean and bright. At night, we came home to a tiny but immaculate, apartment that smelled of frying onions, or a roast beef sputtering in the oven, and Mom, turning from the stove, so happy to see us. It is no small thing to come home to a hot meal, and someone who loves you. Richie was right—home was the best.

"First make tea," was what Mom said when all around us was falling apart, but what she didn't say was what we learned anyway: persevere.

CHAPTER NINE

I FELL IN LOVE WITH PATRICK FRANCIS O'HAGAN, the budding electrical engineer, not only because he was tall, dark, handsome, funny, smart, and had played a bit of football for Manhattan College, but also because on Friday nights, he was willing to take two subway trains and a bus from the Bronx to our Jackson Heights apartment, where he took Richie out of his wheelchair, carried him down the block, up three flights of stairs to visit Pat and Danny O'Rourke and two hours later, back home again, and call it a date.

Long gone were Dad's days of carrying Uncle Willie, Nana, washing machines, and sofas. Dad said that Richie was "dead weight" and so while Dad was at work, or asleep on the sofa with a lit cigarette in his hand, carrying Richie from room to room was mostly Mom's job. "I don't mind," she said, but that was before she developed the second inguinal hernia. Then Dad was forced to get up and help.

It was because of Patrick that Richie loved Friday nights.

He told me that he felt safer in Patrick's arms than in anyone's. Richie asked Patrick to be his Confirmation sponsor, and he even took Patrick's name. Richard Carson Patrick Kehl. It was Patrick who came with me to meet Pam after the church dance where she met Charlie. Like Pam, he was only fifteen, but at six foot seven, he was even taller than Patrick, and in the dark, he looked thirty. Patrick and I stared at him. We followed them all the way home. Charlie might have been taller than Patrick, but Patrick had him by an easy hundred pounds. Charlie still says it was the longest walk of his life. When Patrick came for dinner, sliding into Dad's usually empty place at the table, it was an event. Mom made standing rib roast, lasagna, elaborate stews bubbling under dumpling clouds. And after dinner, when Patrick was there, Mom was in no rush to clear the table. "All wars are economic," he said over the dirty dishes one night, sparking a discussion between the two of them that went on until midnight, and made us miss the movie. "Oh, Christine," Mom said after he'd left, "he's *brilliant*." Forget the words, forget the stories. Patrick was the best thing I'd ever brought home to Mom. "Oh, if only Nana had met him!" Mom said, for my grandmother had died the year before. "She always wanted to marry a tall, dark-haired Irishman like Patrick." I was sixteen. He was nineteen. "Who's half Italian . . ." I reminded her. She waved it away. "Then how come Nana married Pops?" I asked. "A short man with red hair?" "Contrariness," Mom said, putting the platter of meat into the refrigerator.

A year later, Charlie got his driver's license. He and Pam put Richie into his mother's big blue Oldsmobile and brought him to concerts, to Flushing Meadow Park, to the beach, and those were their dates. If it was more than these young men signed on for, they never said. There were no lit cigarettes, and nobody sleeping on the couch. I think of Charlie dragging thousands of dollars worth of Christopher's new computer equipment through the lobby of Hartford Hospital during one of Chris's longer stays, and I think of the World War history lessons Patrick gave Jamie while he was also giving him a bath: the Battle of the Bulge, Vietnam. I stood outside the bathroom door, listening, and holding the towel and when Patrick called "ready!" I'd open the door, and it was like a reverse baptism to see Patrick, wearing the Mets cap he called his "bath hat," pulling his sixty-seven-pound, soaking wet, skeletal son from the tub and I'd think: I hope I was worth it.

Though I was only eighteen in 1968, a year out of high school, and Patrick was barely twenty-one, and still in college, we were saving to get married. Rather, I was saving to get married. Though Patrick had won a full academic scholarship, his part-time job at the college computer center barely covered our movie dates and his engineering textbooks. Ten dollars a week went into a white envelope in my top dresser drawer (for if we wanted a wedding, we'd have to pay for it ourselves), and ten dollars a week went on the kitchen table.

I'd already left the telephone company, where my father had gotten me a job as a "certified name and address" operator, where I wore headphones, and for eight hours a day, matched telephone numbers to names and addresses instead of the other way around, and had gone on to the stock transfer department of Union Carbide on Park Avenue, where, for eight hours a day, by hand, I posted payments to Rockefeller, Kennedy, and Nixon accounts.

It was a lateral move, another ground-level job, but there was overtime at Union Carbide, where Bhopal was still years away, and the job had other perks. Though I never used it, I got a huge discount on insecticide-covered lightbulbs, and "Bugaway" spray. The biggest perk was my young, fun-loving, summertime coworkers, the college kids I envied. If only my father didn't drink so much. If only Mom didn't need my table money. If only we didn't spend so many nights searching for Dad on the empty Jackson Heights streets. If only Richie were normal. If only Mom weren't always so sad, and in such need of cheering up.

In May, when the college kids came tumbling through the revolving doors of Union Carbide, I was an instant young person on a vicarious summer vacation, shedding my winter life like a coat.

It had been so different at the telephone company, where there were no college kids, no summer help. The place was full of grizzled lifers like my father, who were still carrying tool bags, or ancient female "operators" who'd worn headphones for so long (another reason to leave) they sat in the cafeteria with the permanently surprised look of forceps deliveries. The only entertainment to be had at the telephone company was Gretchen Pike, who sat next to me, and suffered from staring fits. Sometimes, she came out of the ladies room wearing only her lacy, hand-embroidered slip, sat down at her desk, put her headphones back on, and stared at the wall. When that happened, our supervisor, Mrs. Krum, herself vacuum-packed into Kimberly knit suits, frantically called Gretchen's brother-in-law, a young executive who had gotten her the job. Waving his Brooks Brothers suit jacket at Gretchen like a bullfighter, and then wrapping her in it, the brother-in-law gently led Gretchen to the door, and the next morning, Gretchen was back at her desk, staring at the wall again as if nothing had happened.

When I looked over at Gretchen Pike, I had no illusions that the telephone company was my fast-track to career success.

May was my favorite Union Carbide month, when the stock transfer department bloomed with college kids, pulling me from the cafeteria that was filled with part-time housewives, out onto the streets for burgers, or pizza, or the "low cal" shakes at Chock Full O'Nuts that were found to have more calories than ice cream. Between the file cabinets in the shipping department, a "colored" college student named "Skippy" (people were yet to become black) taught me to "bugaloo." On coffee breaks, I listened so intently to the English majors talk about novels they'd read that they brought me their old notes, and class syllabuses. They took the Harold Robbins paperbacks out of my hands, and substituted novels by James Baldwin and Truman Capote, which I devoured on the subway ride home from work, more than once looking up and finding myself at Main Street in Flushing, the end of the line. A secondhand education, I told myself, is better than nothing, and an education nonetheless.

In the ladies' lounge one morning before work, I stood in

front of the mirror, staring at the college girls, in their Bass Weejuns loafers, and their simple cotton blouses, sitting on the leather sofa behind me. Everything about them, from their clothes to the easy way they had with each other, seemed to say that they thought they were enough for the world exactly as they were. Then I looked at myself, in my heels, and my tight blouse, a 1960s working-class uniform of too much makeup, too much hair—too "not-enough." I listened to their sorority talk—who was in, who was out, and suddenly, the college life I pined for sounded like the Girl Scouts or the Sodality, and as far from the real world as anyone could get. In my real world, there were no sororities. Too much hair, too much makeup—it didn't matter one way or the other. Richie was up six or seven times a night, calling to be turned over in bed, and Pam and I, despite the seasons, hiding our embarrassing, bouncy breasts in layers of nightgowns, shirts, and blouses, and half-asleep, were fighting bitterly over who had turned him last. One gray dawn, when I'd stumbled out of bed complaining, Richie asked me, out of the blue, "How long do you think I'm going to live?" and it chilled me to my soul. "You're going to live a long time," I said, going back to bed and staring at the ceiling. His arms were now so weak that to feed himself, he had to have his dinner plate propped on the *Webster's Dictionary,* the only thing it seemed good for at the time, for no words could soothe what was happening to him. What does a "sorority" matter when an eleven-year-old brother who sleeps on the other side of his sisters' bedroom, asks how long he has to live?

I stood at the mirror brushing my long, dyed, black

early–Priscilla Presley hairdo and listened for what seemed like the hundredth time to Kathleen's imitation of her father's brogue, and the way he chewed, and how he fussed with his false teeth. This time, unlike the other times, I didn't laugh. I was appalled at how ungrateful she seemed. With his brogue, and his chewing, and his false teeth, Kathleen's father was paying what I considered to be an almost otherworldly steep tuition, and from what she said about him (though I wasn't sure) was sober. She had no idea how lucky she was.

For the first time, it occurred to me that though an education is a privilege, it also involves loss. In a figurative if not literal sense, an education is also a leave-taking, and in a blue-collar family, can have about it the unmistakable whiff of treason. My coworkers might have been more educated than I was, but they were not necessarily any smarter, bragging about their wild parties back at school, and their drinking. Though I listened agreeably and tried to find fun in their stories of throwing up, and waking in strange beds, to me, it sounded like hell. No college had to tell me that alcohol was a brutal killer, turning a father who once made a swing and taught you to fish, into a terrifying stranger, someone you no longer knew. Though painful to endure, an alcoholic rage is really only so much noise. Far worse is the inside out of the thing, how the hidden wounds surface, and gaping, raw pain is out there for all the world to see. In the worst of times, loving an alcoholic means absorbing a few punches to hide all that brokenness, and in the best of times, it's like running for a train that is always pulling out of the station.

And so I promised myself that I would stop accepting the books, and the yellowed course outlines, and stop all the yearning for a life so different from my own. I reapplied my white lipstick, and my black eyeliner, and the hell with it. Though I was vague about the details, I decided I would educate myself by reading books I'd chosen (I knew that the James Baldwin, the Truman Capote, were wonderful beginnings) and in one way or another, live a life that mattered.

And so I made Richie's life into a wonderful story, and the college kids, to my surprise, were mesmerized. I told them that he was in a wheelchair, that he stayed in the bathroom every morning singing the whole *Sgt. Pepper's* album at the top of his lungs. I told them that he'd hidden my blue panty girdle underneath the couch, and I'd had to stay home from school in those pre–panty hose days, with no way to hold up my stockings. I told them that all that pizza for the neighborhood kids, who never had any money, had left me broke. When I talked about Richie, my handicapped brother, I turned it into a performance piece, rolling my eyes, looking up to the heavens. My timing was better than Jack Benny's, and I had so much material to work with. All that spunk, all of his mischievous, indefatigable spirit. (The able-bodied are always dumping mischievous, indefatigable spirit on the disabled. We need it more than they do.) They might have been giving me an education, but I was also giving one to them.

It amazed me that when I came to work in the morning, the college kids, with smiles on their lips, were waiting for me, eager for the next installment. They didn't know anybody who was handicapped. It amazed me that they became as interested in my life as I'd been in theirs. They asked to see

Richie's picture so often that I kept his school picture, with the back of the wheelchair hidden under a dark sheet, in the top drawer of my desk, where I often looked at it myself. Though the real Richie was starting to lose weight, and developing scoliosis, in the picture, with his crazy hair, his freckles all over his face, he looked so normal, like the brother he could have been. If only in a picture, it's sweet to imagine the life you might have had.

When a girl named Brenda told me she was joining the Peace Corps, that she wanted to make a difference, it sounded to me like a life that matters—and I knew exactly what she meant. It was what I felt every time I picked my brother up, sharing the strength I had in my arms, every time I pushed him through the streets, sharing the strength I had in my legs. It seemed to me that using my own life to make someone else's life easier—this was before I realized how easy it is to hide in another's difficult life—was the point. And I didn't have to go off to Africa, I could stay right at home in Jackson Heights.

When the college kids left, my audience was gone, and I missed them. Before I knew it, I was back in the depressing ultramodern Union Carbide cafeteria with the lacquer-haired middle-aged ladies, listening halfheartedly to their recipes, watching them swap coupons. They were so much older than I was, and they'd already made so many choices. If they were asked, maybe they'd say—with children, and grandchildren they seemed only too happy to get away from—that they'd already had lives that mattered, and it wasn't all it was cracked up to be. They didn't want to go to Africa, they wanted to go to the A&P.

Then it was time to leave Union Carbide, get married, and see what real life—including babies, can you imagine that was as much thought as I gave it—and I could offer each other.

CHAPTER TEN

ATRICK AND I WERE MARRIED IN JUNE OF 1970. HE was twenty-two and I was twenty. Five months later, at CBS Television, with my coworkers gathered around the desk, I was in my boss's office when the doctor called to tell me I was pregnant. They shrieked. I cried. When I called Patrick, he cried too. We could hardly pay the rent. The sum total of our worldly possessions were a blue-and-white sofa, a white hurricane lamp we'd bought on our Cape Cod honeymoon, and a bed. *Not a boy,* I prayed, *please God, not a boy.* On my way home from work, I went to Woolworth's, and bought a tiny pair of red booties to keep in my pocket. About a week later, I lost my job. "Nothing personal," Mr. Shepherd said, budget cuts in the ratings department—yet I was the only pregnant employee in our group, and the only one let go. Though I'd had half a dozen jobs, I'd never been fired before. I bolted from his office and ran to the ladies' room where I was so violently sick to my stomach that I could barely stand up. Someone called the nurse, who tried to force me into a wheelchair. "Company policy," she said, yanking on my arm, but I wouldn't budge. Company policy didn't mean a thing to me. My place was behind a wheelchair, not inside one.

Though we barely had a cent, it was sheer heaven to get up in the morning, and turn on the white honeymoon lamp, sit on the blue-and-white sofa, and read the latest selection from the Great Works of Literature Book Club I failed to tell Patrick I'd joined. We barely had groceries in the pantry. On the day that George was telling Lenny about the rabbits, I was so amazed to feel a tiny, tickling crab crawling across the inside of my belly that the book fell from my hands onto the floor. An actual baby after all. A baby girl. It just had to be a girl.

For if they told me that my baby was a boy, I couldn't imagine how I would react. What if I started screaming? What if I went crazy? I had no way of knowing yet how hard it is to go crazy, or how stubborn sanity can be.

When they told me that my baby was a boy, I didn't scream. I'd screamed so much during the delivery that I'd lost my voice. When he came into my room, Patrick had just seen our son. "He's so *dark*," Patrick said, "and his testicles are *huge*," and once more, he burst into tears. I hadn't had much experience with testicles, and didn't know what to make of this news. Then they were putting froggy-eyed Patrick Jr., two weeks early, into my arms. I never knew eight pounds could look so small. Because the curtain was drawn around my bed when my mother came to visit, her nervous system went berserk, and she passed out onto the floor. She came to in the delivery room, after they'd slapped her on a gurney, and raced her down the hall.

Welcome to our family, Patrick Jr.

At the hospital, I spent most of my time at the nursery window. Patrick was the only baby strong enough to hold his head up, and look around the place, as if he were having second thoughts about going home with us, and was looking for the door. The August day we brought him home was very hot. I stood in the doorway, and watched him roll across the bed. Though the pediatrician we brought Patrick to had been Richie's doctor, he didn't seem to remember me. It was his narrow-eyed nurse who stared at me as if I'd been a Nazi during the war. There were a hundred other doctors I could have taken Patrick to, and yet Richie's doctor was as close as I could get to muscular dystrophy's heat, terrified of the flame. "Everything's fine," he said, just as he'd told my mother when Richie was his patient. And no news was still good news.

When Patrick Jr. was born, Richie was a freckle-faced, still somewhat robust-looking fourteen year old. He'd been in the wheelchair for five years, yet he still looked like a sidelined athlete, as if he still might get out. It seemed possible that Mom, with her Irish dreamer's heart, was right when she still insisted that Richie would "someday" be cured. Pam and I still never asked about this cure. "How long do we have to wait?" I wanted to ask, but never did. It felt cruel to press Mom. Her life was so hard. She never stopped caring for Richie, she never stopped worrying about Dad. In my heart, I knew that Mom didn't have the answer, that she was as hungry as we were for the crumbs of hope she fed us, and they tasted so good. I told myself that the party we'd had on the day Richie came home from the hospital was nothing compared to the party we'd have on the day he started to walk again.

When Patrick was six months old, hardly ready to stand, I stood him in his carriage facing away from me, with his hands on the carriage hood, and paraded him through the Jackson Heights streets—just in case I was to meet someone who knew our family, and might be tempted to ask if he was "okay." Although muscular dystrophy wouldn't show up yet for years, I wanted everyone in the world to see this beautiful son, healthy beyond health itself. Six months old, and already bearing the burden of proof.

By the time Patrick was seven months old, Richie was in a huge, motorized wheelchair he'd gotten from the Muscular Dystrophy Association.

On the day it was delivered, he waited for me, on the corner, under the el. I could see his grin a block away. The closer I got, however, the tinier he looked, stuck deeper in disability than I'd ever thought possible, more and more powerless in his new "power" chair, and it was finally clear to me that he was sidelined for good. "Look at this!" he called, speeding toward us, speeding away, making wide circles, leaving faint rubber tracks on the sidewalk, showing off. It was almost unbearable to see how happy he was. There's no going back, I thought, for a motorized wheelchair is as permanent as a headstone. He sped away from us, taking with him any hope I'd ever had of this mystical "cure." The simple truth was that Richie would never get any better.

———

Only then did it occur to me that although I was doing all I could think of to keep Patrick Jr. healthy and safe in the world, even stopping at the corners of busy streets and taking him out of the carriage and holding against my chest, under my antique raccoon coat, in case a car were to go out of control, muscular dystrophy could be going on inside of him anyway. He wasn't yet a year old. I didn't think I was strong enough to live with the knowledge that I had passed muscular dystrophy on to my beautiful, innocent son.

And then one day on Queens Boulevard, after we'd successfully crossed the street, after I'd taken Patrick out from underneath my thick coat, after I'd put him back in the carriage, a workman's hammer fell from the subway tracks above our heads, bounced off the carriage hood, and skidded along the street.

It's pitiful how little we can control.

When Patrick Jr. was a toddler, I didn't worry about DMD. I was too busy chasing him. "I've seen active children," my mother smiled, "but this child is beyond the beyonds . . ." and it was true. He jumped in and out of his carriage. In our big, empty apartment, he disappeared. He got into closets and shut the door, waded in the toilet, ate a tube of Avon's "Woody Rose" lipstick, sprayed his tongue with dry shampoo. He scaled the refrigerator, ate a whole bottle of Flintstone's vitamins, climbed into the sink. It feels as though I spent the entire early seventies running down the corridor of our gloomy apartment, shrieking Patrick's name. On TV, and in print, feminists told me that my housewife/mother life was "oppressive," but to me, it didn't feel that way. It was a life that mattered, and I was bedazzled by it. In what other circumstances, I asked myself, could I have found this deep a love in what felt like this holy a life? It was like suddenly discovering that I could turn cartwheels, or speak Russian. The naps, the baby foods, the tiny white shirts drying on the clothesline were seed pearls sewn into organdy days, baby powder everywhere like fairy dust. Patrick Jr. was overwhelmingly healthy. Luck seemed to be with us, and I wanted to try again, just one more time, another little person to love.

"But we really can't afford it yet," Patrick Sr. said. Wearing his undershirt, with his black hair falling into his eyes, Patrick was sitting at the old, paint-splattered table his Aunt Mae had given us, eating my spongy pancakes. Afford? That sounded terrible to me. Patrick was a junior engineer with a bright future. That he was not yet twenty-five with a family to support didn't seem unfair to me. I was too busy living a life that mattered. Patrick seemed older, saner, more responsible than I would someday know the age of twenty-five to be. His biggest vice was his corncob pipe, tightly packed with Captain Black tobacco, a scent that made me think of my grandfather and feel safe. Making me feel safe was Patrick's job.

"But don't expect me to help a lot," he cautioned, "I have to keep my job," and I nodded. I didn't expect him to help at all. His job was to go to work, and mine was all the rest. This didn't strike me as unfair either. I was young, and strong, and eager to give another baby everything I had—which should have been a warning, but wasn't. Like me, my playground girlfriends were all in their early twenties, and on to their second babies.

"I wanted to get it over with," some of them said of their second pregnancies, exactly what they said about deliberately exposing their babies to the chicken pox. They told me it was good to have babies close together, as if I were on the same playing field as they were, with their football-baseball-basketball-playing brothers, the lady-killers they bragged about. When my mother pushed Richie to the park, it was as if the playground girlfriends had never seen a wheelchair before, and they stared at his wheelchair, his misshapen back and his pale, gaunt face, and though I hated myself for it, I was embarrassed. I wondered if they'd make the connection, perhaps look at Patrick Jr. differently, realize by looking at my brother, the terrible chance I had already taken, and was thinking of taking again. One cold Saturday, when Richie was home with Dad, and Patrick Jr. was home with Patrick, my mother and I were strolling along Thirty-seventh Avenue, when I suddenly told her that I would accept any child God would give me as long as Patrick, my first, was healthy. She stopped dead in the street, stared into my eyes, and for the longest time, stood with her leather-gloved hand clamped over my mouth.

On Christmas night, 1972, after cooking my first turkey dinner for our families, and feeling very married, I got out of bed to cover sixteen-month-old Patrick, asleep in his crib, and get a drink of water, and I knew I was pregnant. *Now you've done it,* I thought, and pushed the thought away. Patrick Jr. was healthy, Cousin Grace had all those healthy boys, and there was a 50 percent possibility that I might have a girl. It wouldn't be until *she* was ready to have kids, maybe another twenty years or so, and DMD would surely be cured by then—that we'd even have to think about it again. It was on Valentine's Day that the news became official. I was pregnant again. I left the doctor's office and called Patrick from a pay phone on Northern Boulevard. "Great!" Patrick said, but he was in a rush. Instead of worrying about DMD, I worried instead that I could never love another baby as much as I loved Patrick, never suspecting the elasticity of a mother's heart.

At twenty-three years old, robustly pregnant, using the healthy body God had blessed me with to its greatest advantage, I felt that I was spending it all, whatever currency I had in this life, and it had nothing to do with money, or possessions, of which we still had very little. One of Aunt Mae's paint-splattered chairs was banished to the living room, where it sat in a corner holding our TV, under a stretched-out wire coat hanger instead of an antenna. When Patrick came home at night, wearing his white canvas coat, his face flushed from the cold, Patrick Jr., my belly, and I were waiting for him at the top of the stairs. With the mail in his hands, he looked up at us and grinned. Sometimes our downstairs neighbor, the elegant, widowed, ancient Mr. Kroski, who worried about the baby, and stayed up at night fixing the furnace, was right in back of Patrick, carrying a Bohack bag, which I imagined held a single lamb chop. Mr. Kroski smiled and waved. Though I couldn't be sure, I suspected that the journey from a young family waiting at the top of the stairs to a single chop in a Bohack bag was a short one.

We were so sure our second baby was going to be a girl that we bought pink kimonos, and painted the room pink. We would call "her" "Alanna," an Irish name that is a term of endearment, like "sweetheart" or "darling," a name that I wrote with great flourish whenever I got my hands on a pen, and a grocery bag, a name that I wrote in the margins of the *Daily News,* or on the backs of envelopes, all those peaking *a*'s and soft *n*'s.

Named for his maternal great-grandfather, my beloved Pops, and his paternal grandfather who'd died the year before he was born, James Owen was born on September 20, 1973, on the night that tennis champ Billie Jean King beat Bobby Riggs in their much-publicized match. Jamie was nearly ten pounds, and his birth the hardest, most strenuous physical work I've ever done. His birth made Patrick Jr.'s birth seem about as painful as dental X-rays. Minutes after Jamie was born, the nurses temporarily left us alone, sneaking into the next room to see Billie Jean King's press conference. It was all noise to me. "Hi," I said to my big beautiful baby. Pink-cheeked, blue-eyed, fair, Jamie was a baby confection, a marzipan, who somehow managed to look like a cross between Paul Newman and Alfred Hitchcock, and nothing at all like his dark-haired, olive-skinned older brother. Jamie looked up at me, and stuck his tongue out.

Home from the hospital on a chilly fall day, Jamie brought the winter of 1973–1974 with him. His breasts were engorged with milk that some called "witches' brew." To get him to drink from his bottle, I first had to brush his lips with my pinkie. Even then, he hated to have anything in his mouth. We'd been home only for a few hours when two-year-old

Patrick Jr. somehow took the baby out of his bassinet, and was running with him down the hall. With our second baby, on our first day home, we bought a hook and eye for his bedroom door.

The first week that Jamie was home, Pam and Charlie got engaged. They came over to show me the ring. Patrick was working overtime, the washing machine was filled with diapers, the baby's bottles were on the stove, in the sterilizer, right next to the boiling spaghetti. The kitchen floor was slippery with Weebils, the baby was screaming, and Patrick Jr., who had an ear infection, was clinging to my knees.

"This is what you're getting into," I said, the older, wiser sister, never suspecting that we were all getting into much, much worse.

"Maybe I should reconsider," Charlie laughed, and Pam poked him in his belly.

CHAPTER ELEVEN

LTHOUGH HE DID EVERYTHING THAT PATRICK HAD done, Jamie was very different from Pat. Patrick was dark eyed, with wiry dark hair and a cleft in his chin. Jamie was fair, blue-eyed, his hair a silky auburn, with three skinny dimples, like commas, on each side of his mouth. Patrick was excitable and intense. Jamie was placid and unruffled. Patrick was afraid of clowns, Santa Claus, the bogeyman, lightning, thunder, hail, stray dogs, alley cats, mangy little squirrels at the park—but not Jamie. Nothing bothered Jamie. When he was about a year old, an old yellow-toothed horse in front of Central Park rammed his head into Jamie's stroller. Three-year-old Patrick shrieked, and hid behind me, but Jamie simply smiled at the horse, and patted his nose. It wasn't so much that the boys looked nothing alike, or that they had such different temperaments, or even that Jamie was so much smaller, thinner, slighter than Patrick. After all, there were two years between them, and not everyone in our mixed-up gene pool was big. If someone had asked to explain the real difference between my sons, I'd have said that Jamie had a hesitation about him, and was, in some inexplicable way, one beat behind Pat.

Since Patrick Sr. didn't think that Jamie was "one beat, two beats, or any 'beats' at all behind Pat," and my mother told me I was "looking for trouble," and nobody else said anything, I put Jamie's hesitation out of my mind, and waited for someone else to point out what was wrong—and it was the father at the kiddie birthday party, a well-meaning but dopey man, who did. My moment of knowing. Our old pediatrician had retired. Without sharing our family history, we found a new pediatrician who joked with Patrick Jr. while he was examining Jamie, and to my huge relief, found nothing wrong. No news was still good news, good enough, for me.

So until that hesitation explained itself, I responded to Jamie in the way he seemed to need responding to. While Patrick was scaling the back of the sofa, leaping across our queen-size bed, Jamie was watching from the doorways, or putting his arms up to me. Whenever I sat down, he crawled into my lap. My mother warned me that I was making him "a lap baby," and his "immaturity" was my fault, but I knew instinctively that the hesitation was still there, and I never said no. I held him as much as he needed to be held. Each minute he was in my arms was a minute less that he was on the floor, being one beat behind Pat. Though I knew they had bought us time, I gave away the carriage, and I gave away the stroller, and I agreed with Patrick and my mother, who said we didn't need them anymore, with Jamie walking everywhere, even if he never alternated feet on the stairs, and ran ever so slowly. I told myself that the boys were just different. Patrick was sweet, and cooperative, and Jamie was sweet but quirky. Though his third birthday was still months away, I'd spent one solid week singing "Happy Birthday" to Jamie as soon as he opened his eyes, letting him blow out the single candle in the chocolate cupcake I'd let him have for breakfast—or else he'd slump to the floor in a teary wad of grief. Patrick sat perfectly still for his first haircut but when I brought Jamie to the barber for the first time, he was so furious he wiggled out of the barber's chair and ran out the door with one side of his head shaved, and the other side, reddish, shoulder-length curls that stayed that way for almost a month. One night, Jamie climbed out of his crib—funny how the one night that Jamie did this stands out against the 3,000 nights that Patrick did the same thing—crept into my bedroom, got into my purse. When I got to the doorway to see what he was up to, he whirled around, and his eyelashes were covered with my mascara. He looked like someone from *A Clockwork Orange*.

In nursery school, Patrick got into fights, but Jamie's classmates fed the hesitation that I sensed, three and four year olds tucking their bananas, or their cookies, into his schoolbag. Terence's mother told me that at home, Terence had said Jamie was "an itty-bitty boy," but when she saw Jamie, she was surprised to see that he was as big as all the rest. When I bent down to talk to Jamie, he listened not by looking at me, but by squinting into the distance, as if he were reading from a teleprompter. Screaming at Patrick to stop at the corners, I dragged Jamie through the Jackson Heights streets, yet when Jamie got to kindergarten, he managed, just like the other kids, to climb three flights of stairs to his classroom, and back down again. Though there were some days that he came through that heavy door holding the teacher's hand, there weren't many.

Sometimes, I wonder what I was doing on the day when Jamie was as strong as he would ever be, for in every illness, there has to be that last day before the evil cells begin to divide, or the heart begins to sputter. With his hand snug in mine, did Jamie "peak" somewhere along Northern Boulevard, amid the rust and the trucks, or did he "peak" while we were walking underneath the crumbling Brooklyn-Queens Expressway? Was it while we were at C-Town buying groceries, or getting Patrick's dry cleaning for yet another business trip? Perhaps Jamie "peaked" on one of those sunny afternoons when Patrick was still in school, and Jamie was sitting calmly on the striped living-room rug watching *Sesame Street*, while I laid on the sofa with another migraine, and a cold cloth over my eyes, days that in retrospect seem way too many.

If Jamie peaked, he did so quietly. He grew into a fun-loving, easygoing, giggling little boy who seems now to have been too wonderfully ordinary for all that would be asked of him. Patrick was the idealist, Jamie was the realist. In his twelfth summer, when my leg was in a cast, and Patrick Sr. was traveling all over the country, it was almost impossible for me to give Jamie a bath. "Oh Jamie," I'd cried, standing at the side of the bathtub, fiddling with the towel and trying to balance myself, "how are we going to get through this life?" to which he calmly replied, "Well, the first step is to get me out of the tub." When I asked five-year-old Patrick what he wanted to be when he grew up, he said "fireman, baseball player, policeman, doctor," while Jamie just looked at him. "What about you?" I asked Jamie. "Big," he said, the single goal that nevertheless eluded him.

In school, Jamie printed his name not as "James Owen," but as "James Own." When Patrick and I told him he was our "one and only Own, the only Own we own," he laughed, delightedly squishing his fingers together, as if he were barely able to stand being so happy.

If only we had owned him. As all parents come to learn, fate is the real custodial parent.

But how I wish we could have some of that one peaking day back, even if it was only for a quick sprint on roller skates, or a two-minute ride on a new bike.

Ah, sweet Richie, that bright, happy baby, whose face was filled with a million possibilities. Although there were only seven years between us, when Richie was born, some window of my young soul flew open, and everything seemed nicer somehow, sweeter, clearer, and for the first time, I thought *so this is what it is to love*. And when Richie got sick, it hurt more than I could have imagined. Sore inside from the age of nine, or ten, when it was clear that something terrible was wrong, I was surprised to see the other side of love—there was no going back to that pre-Richie place.

In the fifties, and even into the early sixties when the demographics changed, Jackson Heights, Queens, felt like a storybook place. Once known as "A Garden in the City," it was America's first "garden and cooperative community," in a part of Queens that had once been farmland, and evolved into a leisurely, beautiful neighborhood, designed by then-famous architects and filled with brick English garden homes with slate roofs, and small front lawns lush with ivy, lilac, daffodils. At one time, there were tennis courts, and green-and-white-striped awnings covering the windows of the brick apartment buildings that were all built around elaborate courtyards, in which there were gardens filled with stone sculpture, ornamental ironwork, gushing fountains. In the lobbies, not only were there uniformed doormen but there were paintings on the walls, Oriental carpeting on the shiny wood floors, and working fireplaces. Eighty-second Street was the shopping hub, cotton shops, and jewelry shops, and tiny elegant bakeries. Ah Jackson Heights, it wasn't you I fled, but the memories, for as Richie declined, you declined for me too, and the streets where I'd found so much of your charm, from the brass kickplates and doorknobs on the front doors, to the pots of violets on the enameled windowsills under spotless windows full of lacy, cris-cross curtains, were the same streets that ended in high curbs Richie couldn't climb, and too many places where he'd fallen down, cracked his head, lost his baby tooth, scraped his elbow, cut his knee. Your streets are still a sacred battlefield to me, Richie's own Antietam, where, if I looked hard enough, I think I might still find traces of my poor brother's blood.

Or maybe I was looking for the geographic cure, with Jamie one beat behind Pat. At any rate, I had to get out. Pam and Charlie were already gone, living upstate in Olean, New York, with Chris and Jason, who were babies. In his wheelchair, on those fading Jackson Heights streets, Richie was barely able to hold up his head. It was too much. It was too hard to look at Richie, it was too easy to remember all that pain.

And that was how Patrick and I found ourselves in the sales office of a model home on Long Island, signing a binder for a one-story house that we told each other Richie could move around in when he came to visit—a half truth. ("You can't put an old head on young shoulders," was all my mother would say of this idea, although the first time she'd come to visit, she'd stand stock-still on the deadly quiet, sunny suburban street, and scream *"Visiting day at the institution!"* to no one in particular.) Though Patrick and I wanted a home of our own, and the boys in a better school, what I wanted more—and never told my mother—was a brand-new life in a brand-new place, even though I didn't know how I could ever leave my brother, who'd graduated from Human Resources School and had even managed a few college courses before it all became too much for him, and he was homebound. It was a miracle he was still alive. He adored Patrick and Jamie, and every day, after school, I brought them to see him. Uncle Rich kept a "goody bag" of toys in his bedroom closet, and a stack of board games underneath his bed. Although he could no longer use his hands, the kids moved the game board pieces for him. Patrick was a quick study, and when he was only seven, Richie had taught him to play poker—though Patrick was at an advantage, holding both his and Richie's hands. The kids were a gift I brought to my brother, and my mother. There was no other way I could think of to ease their housebound days—and when my father came home, their sad nights—all strung together like socks on a line. I couldn't give Richie mobility, health, strength, but I could bring my children to him, little bits of boys, with their school projects, and their homework pages, their missing teeth, and their grimy fingers, and the puppy-dog smell of their hair, and my brother got it, and laughed at them, and loved them. That they might need kids their own ages, or some time at the playground (especially for Jamie, with his walking days drawing to a close) was something that I thought of—but dismissed. Our new house would be ready in a year, and from the looks of the suburban neighborhood, plenty of kids for ours to play with. By then, I hoped I'd be able to leave Queens, and Richie, who needed us so much.

In the meantime, on the after-school afternoons when Richie was up to it, we were off to the five and ten for hotdogs, or to Papa Jahn's for ice cream: Mom, Richie, Patrick Jr., Jamie, and I. On the fifteenth of the month, Richie's Social Security check came in and then we were off to Toy City. For Patrick's First Communion, Richie bought him a baseball glove, looking over it as carefully as if he had been Joe DiMaggio. Mom and I took turns pushing the wheelchair, the kids holding on to either side. When people stared at us, as people inevitably did, Patrick and Jamie glared at them. When it was my mother's turn to push the wheelchair, there was something about her sensible nurse's shoes, and the whiff of pine cleaner from her durable clothing, and her Irish determination that made me feel strangled. Between the two of us, there was so much responsibility that I wanted to run away, jump on one of those buses, head into New York and whatever I might find there. The life that mattered sometimes felt like a yoke around my neck. My mother hadn't gotten married until she was almost thirty. By the time I'm thirty, I told my-self, I'll be married ten years. *I haven't had enough life.* And yet when I looked at my brother, I was ashamed—Richie had hardly any life left.

Sometimes, Patrick Sr. was angry that I spent so much time with my mother and my brother. It was as if I'd never left home, he said, and he was sick of it. The boys should be out playing with other kids, he said, and on weekends, we should be spending more time together, as a family, just the four of us; but then Saturday nights came along, and there we were, at my parents' apartment, eating ice cream, watching TV. Although he didn't want to, Patrick understood. "We'll be gone soon enough," I'd cry, but I never thought that Richie would be gone first.

CHAPTER TWELVE

N JULY OF 1979, A MONTH BEFORE OUR NEW HOUSE was ready, Richie caught a summer cold that became pneumonia. He was twenty-two years old. When Dr. Oh, his tiny Korean doctor, came to the apartment, he picked Richie up in his arms, and headed for the door. There were no biPAPs or vents in those days to help DMD boys breathe. "Please," Dr. Oh said, "only three blocks to hospital" but Richie didn't want to go to the hospital, or be carried through the streets. He wanted to stay home. Home was the best. Against his better judgment, Dr. Oh gave Richie prescriptions, and his home telephone number just in case. At three in the morning, Richie couldn't breathe, and while my father slept, my mother got Richie into the wheelchair, and ran the three blocks to the hospital, where they gave him oxygen, and rushed him to the ICU, where no kids were allowed. Only one adult at a time could visit Richie, and only for ten minutes every hour. In the thin hospital gown, his emaciated body—a back ballooned by scoliosis, arms and legs as skinny and gnarled as the branches of an olive tree—was shocking. He couldn't talk to me, he was struggling too hard to breathe, the oxygen mask little more than a grain of sand against the tide, and then my ten minutes were up. I left the hospital. An hour later, when I came back, I was getting on the elevator, and my father was getting off. I hurled myself at him and he was barely able to stand up under my assault. "He'll be fine," my father said, pulling away from me and out through the revolving door. In the ICU upstairs, Richie was on a respirator. Fully conscious, on your back, unable to move with a respirator tube stuck in your throat has to be in the top ten—if not the top two—of all possible horrendous experiences. And not being able to say a word. A big piece of oaktag, on which a sweet young nurse had printed the alphabet in big, loopy letters, was how we communicated: one letter at a time, and Richie would either nod, or roll his huge, dark eyes. It was time consuming, but it gave us something to do, and it was better than listening to the respirator's hiss. "Where's my forty dollars?" was the first thing he "asked" me, for he was always lending me money, and then I was relieved. He was still Richie, and I wanted to think he'd get better.

One morning, he looked up at me, and started to spell, but "I lov . . ." was as far as he got before I stopped him, holding my hand like a traffic cop's. When Richie was eight months old, my father had taken the two of us to Rockaway Beach, where for the first time, I'd had the baby all to myself, and had nuzzled his neck, his duckling blond hair peeking out from underneath the hood of his yellow-and-white beach towel. I was eight years old, and it was the first perfect moment I'd ever had. I could still feel his baby weight in my arms. "Don't tell me that!" I snapped, twenty-nine years old and I should have known better.

Richie looked at me, and rolled his eyes. I don't know if he ever forgave me. Into the wounded space between us, I fit an anecdote—Patrick Jr. had lost his new blue sneaker some-where in the sandy foundation of our half-built house. Richie knew how clumsy Patrick was, a huge puppy of a kid, with big feet he was always tripping over, big hands he didn't quite know what to do with, a spiller of milk, a loser of things, and Richie smiled. I never told Richie, or anyone else, that one pastel winter dusk, when Patrick was fourteen months old, and sleepy, that I took him out of the stroller and watched in horror as he fell to the ground, and couldn't seem to get up. What would he have thought, what would Patrick Sr. have thought, or any of the neighbors, had they seen me standing my baby, then pushing him down just to see him get up again. His little face lost its color. He stared at me in disbelief, and cried, his mouth a perfect *o*. It wasn't until much later that I realized he'd simply outgrown his snowsuit, too snug in the crotch.

Never alone a day in his life, Richie died by himself. Born on a Saturday, and died on a Saturday. My mother was at the supermarket when it happened, and my father was alone when he got the call. When I came through the door, carrying Patrick Jr.'s First Communion pictures, Dad was sitting in the flowered chair by the open window, next to the white wicker table. "It's all over," was all he said to me, and then he burst into tears, smashing the wicker table with his fist. I'd like to say that I went over to him, put my arms around him, embraced him—but I did none of that. I was afraid of making things worse. I didn't want the be the one who'd "set him off." Addicts protect themselves from their feelings, but the rest of us, no matter how we protest, are complicit. When my mother opened the door, she took one look at us, dropped the bag of groceries on the floor, sagged against the door frame—but I didn't go to her either. I knew my mother, and I knew she would push me away. What kind of family was ours? Then my mother's friend Dolores came to the apartment, and told us that we had tried so hard, and had given Richie the best life possible. Nobody had ever said that to us before. We didn't think anybody had noticed. It wasn't until we embraced Dolores—another spark to follow—that we were able to embrace one another. My father, who never understood subtleness, and could never see the world's plentiful gray, sent a broken heart of red roses to the funeral home. On Long Island a month before we were, Richie's in Calverton Cemetery, with too many Vietnam vets. After the funeral, wearing black clothing in the middle of summer, with nowhere else to go, we stopped at the new house, and walked through the newly framed rooms. With Patrick's sneaker somewhere in the bowels of the house, it was as if we already had one foot in our new life.

CHAPTER THIRTEEN

T NONE OF OUR AFTERNOON GET-TOGETHERS DID I
tell my new Long Island neighbors that I'd just lost
my brother. They didn't even know I'd had a brother.
I said I'd had a younger married sister, and she and her family
lived upstate, although it felt odd, for Calverton Cemetery
was a lot closer than Olean, New York. Richie was the one
who was practically right next door. Although Patrick and
Jamie had been with their uncle all of their lives, they seldom
asked about him. If they did, I simply repeated what I'd said
on the day that Richie died. He'd been sick, and had gone to
heaven where he was now happy—although Patrick Jr., at
eight, was old enough to know that Richie had seemed happy
enough, wheelchair or not, playing board games, on earth—
but what else is there to say? I wondered if they were "too
young" to miss him. Then one day, Patrick came in from playing football, and sat in the kitchen chair across the table from
where I sat peeling potatoes. "What exactly happens when
someone dies?" he asked. "They go on to another kind of life,"

I said. He nodded, and went back outside. If there wasn't much talk about Richie on Long Island, there was no talk about him at all back in Queens. When we were visiting my parents, I tried to talk about him, but then my mother looked pointedly at my father, and at me, a warning finger brushing her lips. The subject was off limits. Mom didn't want to send Dad to the bar any sooner, or to the bottle any deeper. When Dad left the room, Mom whispered that she didn't want to "set him off." Instead, she brought all of us into Richie's old room—where the children stood close to Patrick and me, their heads buried in our thighs, their eyes closed except to peek at the closet where their games and toys had so recently been— to see the new maple bedroom set. The hospital bed, the two wheelchairs, the hoya lift, the hospital tray, the gobs of lamb's wool were gone, and the freshly painted bedroom seemed so empty that the new bedroom set, like my parents themselves, looked tiny and lost. We admired the new ivory-and-cream Oriental carpets instead, the new coffee table, the new end tables covered in Irish lace—all the furniture that having a wheelchair in a small apartment forbids. (They even bought an artificial fireplace that they turned on, like Richard Nixon, in the middle of the summer.) Though Pam and I had stood together in front of Richie's casket, just as we had stood in front of his crib, we never talked about him. Patrick was eight, Jamie, almost six, Chris was three and Jason two. Silence was the only way we tried to keep muscular dystrophy away.

It was the Irish writer C. S. Lewis who wrote that grief feels so much like fear, and on Long Island, in the beginning, I was afraid of everything. There were fathomless black nights, and sunlight so intense that it made everyone crazy, and made me think of city roaches, scattering across the kitchen counters the minute the light is turned on. The sky looked like the ocean, and the ocean looked like the sky. Nobody on our street had any fences, and I was afraid of the deer jumping across the backyard, and the packs of mangy dogs emerging from the woods. I was afraid of the fierce-looking Indians, in their bright, homemade ponchos, and their black hair in long braids, who left the nearby reservation and drove through our streets, selling homemade wooden furniture from the backs of pickup trucks. I was afraid of the nighttime bonfires that some of the neighbors set. I was afraid of the raccoons, the mice, the squirrels, the opossums, the snakes, the frogs, the goddamn flora and fauna of it all. (What I was most terrified of was my brother, in his navy blue burial suit, stepping out of the woods, and accusing me of abandoning him.)

When the Welcome Wagon lady, wearing an embroidered smock, ankle socks, shiny black Mary Janes, with her hair in long blond braids, and carrying a willow basket filled with samples and coupons, rang my doorbell, it struck me as so funny that I had to leave the poor woman sitting at my kitchen table, run into the bathroom, and press one of the new hand towels against my mouth. We were all young, blue-collar women from Brooklyn, or Queens. We might as well have had Glinda the Good Witch, or Little Red Riding Hood standing at our front doors. *"The fucking Welcome Wagon lady!"* my next-door neighbor Paula said, and as we laughed at this storybook idea that had found us, I felt my terrible fear— and my grief—lessen just a bit. Month by month, I felt a little lighter, a little less afraid. There were so many new houses and so many new babies (all the garbage-day effluvia of those reproductive years, the condoms, the sanitary pads big as softballs, the used Pampers blowing around in the gutter) that I began to feel slowly, very slowly, reinvented, and for practically the first time in my life—though guilty as hell over it—anonymous. What brother in the wheelchair? As far as anyone on Long Island knew, we were just another normal couple with two normal little boys. With my brother gone, I didn't feel compelled to live a life that mattered anymore. Like Susan's, like Janie's, like Paula's, like Cindy's, mine was just a life. Sitting in my new friends' kitchens, sipping tea, eating cookies, I felt younger than I'd ever felt—as if I were going backward, and starting over again. I was twenty-nine years old, away from my parents, my brother, and for the first time in my life, that whole sad past. So much freedom was intoxicating.

If only Jamie wasn't having such a hard time climbing onto the school bus.

CHAPTER FOURTEEN

I T'S BECAUSE HE'S SO SHORT, I SAID ON THAT FIRST day of school, to anyone who'd listen, feeling the panic rising in my throat. Although he was as tall as the other first graders leaping in front of him, cutting him off, sometimes knocking him off his feet, the other mothers at the bus stop agreed. "Aw, give him a little time," someone said, "in a week, he'll be flying up those steps. You'll see . . ." *Please God, please. Not again.* When Jamie flopped into the seat by the window, smiled and waved, smashed his freckled nose against the dirty glass, crossed his eyes, we all laughed. It was impossible not to. He was adorable. He'll get taller, I told myself, everything will be fine. In the blazing sunshine, Jamie and I sat on the front porch, watching Patrick and the other kids wrestling, running, skating all over the struggling lawns. I rubbed Jamie's back, and told myself that all I had to do was wait. When Richie was six, we knew there was something wrong. Jamie was six, and still able to "pass." I didn't tell myself to take him to the doctor already and get it over with, that either he had MD, or he didn't, that it's too much agony not to know. I couldn't face it. Though it never occurred to me to take credit for Patrick's incredible health—who would do that?—I felt 100 percent to blame for Jamie's troubles, and I was so scared. It was the most terrible time of my life. And I didn't talk it over with my mother, who was just getting over Richie's death, or with Pam, who had two little boys of her own to worry about. And though Patrick Sr. knew that Jamie was "struggling a little" with the school bus, I didn't tell him how hard it really was, how terrified I felt. He was an innocent in all this, and I wanted to somehow spare him. He'd already had enough DMD to last a lifetime. He'd never gone to the bus stop, never seen how Jamie struggled, didn't know what an ordeal it was. Unfortunately, I couldn't hide Jamie's trouble from Patrick Jr., who was only eight years old, and couldn't be spared at all. He was too smart not to know that something was wrong, that it was something we needed to hide. You'd think he was clowning around when he so quietly and competently grabbed Jamie by the hand, and yanked him up those stairs. My best friend Ruthie, who lived forty miles away, was the only one I talked to about Jamie. "Take him to the doctor," Ruthie urged, "I'll even go with you," but this seemed sneaky, going behind Patrick's back, and I just couldn't do it. I was too scared to actually *do* anything—but wait. And pray. And tell Ruthie, over and over again, that only a few months earlier he'd gone up and down those sooty, kindergarten steps, and in such a short time, how much could change? "He's probably fine," Ruthie said, which made me feel a little bit better.

When I was finally brave enough to visit Jamie's teacher, and ask how he was doing, she said that he was "immature" and that a lot of kids had a hard time climbing onto the school bus, especially kids who've come from the city, and have never been on a school bus in their lives, and that he'd grow out of it. He might be a little less active than the other kids, but then he was a "phlegmatic" kind of kid anyway, and she'd had a lot of those, the ones who wouldn't move very fast even if the building were on fire. "But he's very determined," she said, "at recess, he stays by himself, and pulls himself up and down that slide at least a dozen times. I think he's practicing," she smiled, and although I felt sick to my stomach, I smiled back. "You might work on his fine motor skills," she said, "encourage him to use scissors, and clay." Now that was something different—nobody ever said anything about Richie's "fine motor skills." Maybe I was worrying about muscular dystrophy, and it was a "fine motor skills" disorder all the while. He could live with that, and so, I thought, could we. We bought him scissors, modeling clay, finger paints, water paints, rolls of white paper, oaktag, paintbrushes, Play-Doh, and let him spread everything all over the kitchen floor. And he drew pictures of superheroes, painted, made clay and Play-Doh figurines that were surprisingly lifelike—but he still struggled to climb the bus stairs.

A month later, while we were waiting for Jamie's "maturity" to kick in, I carried him onto the bus in the morning and sat him in his seat, and when the bus got to school, Patrick helped him off. At 3:00, it was Patrick's turn to help Jamie on to the bus, and my turn to be at the bus stop to help him off. My neighbors were complaining that their kids were up and down the stairs so much that their sneakers were always ruined, and there were holes in the builder's thin carpeting. When I noticed worn spots in our carpet, or holes in Patrick's sneakers, I said a grateful Hail Mary, bought small throw rugs, threw the sneakers out. I had to hold Jamie's sneakers up to the light to see any wear. "Worn sneakers are a gift," I wanted to say, but normal people wouldn't know what I was talking about.

And it went on like this for a year. A year of visiting the neighbors, in the afternoons, for tea. A year of the kids coming home from school, and playing on the lawns. A year of watching Patrick, who was always the first one tired of playing outside, coming through the door. A year of wondering where Jamie was. A year of watching Jamie settling himself onto those family-room carpets by crouching and then falling the rest of the way. A year of seeing Jamie in the family rooms watching TV by himself, when Patrick and the other kids had gone on to something else, something that was usually upstairs. A year of trying to be a normal mother and wife, interested in throw pillows, curtains, coupons while watching Jamie, through the doorway, struggle to get up from the floor, and find the others. He was trying to pass as a regular kid, I was trying to pass as a regular mother. The new happy family I was trying to present to the world was, in fact, the same old sad family. All that was changed were the sur-roundings. When it was too painful to watch Jamie struggle to stand, I got up, went into those family rooms, pulled Jamie to his feet, and we set off together to find the other kids. Up the stairs, with me right behind him. We were halfway up the flight, but instead of Mrs. O'Brien, or the Meenahan bride, trying to pass by, there was a roaring tide of kids com-ing down. Embarrassed by my constant, hovering presence, Patrick glared at me, but Jamie was grateful. "Thanks, Mom," he whispered, before turning around, and taking my hand for the trip back down. I was so relieved when Jamie was in the family room, with all the kids are around him, and he was not alone. When I came back to the table, everyone laughed at how neurotic I was, and they all bet I'd be follow-ing Jamie and Patrick through college classrooms, business meetings, and there on their wedding nights. It was easier when the kids were actually in the house. Sometimes they disappeared from the lawns, leaving Jamie all by himself, with no one to come and get me if he fell. Then Jamie came looking for me, and the hostess of whichever house I was in, opened the front door for him, and waited for him to pull himself up the steps. I didn't run to the door, for to leap up and drag him inside would only make me seem even crazier, and Jamie, more "abnormal." And so I sat frozen in my chair, staring at the back of Cindy or Janie or Paula or Susan, wait-ing so patiently for my son, who was such a nice boy, and didn't deserve any of it. I wished I were any of them, with all those wild, healthy children. "Take your time," they sometimes kidded Jamie, and ever the good sport, he laughed—and so did I. The bugs rushed in, the warm or cool air rushed out and Jamie plodded on, climbing the concrete steps, one foot at a time.

"Maybe he needs glasses," the teacher suggested, somewhere in that year, and I practically fell on her I was so relieved. And sure enough, he was nearsighted—like I am—but the new glasses didn't help his coordination, his immaturity, his fine motor skills. "There's something wrong," I whispered to Patrick, late one night, in bed. "Please take him to the doctor," Patrick said, and left for work. On a brilliant autumn morning, a week after I'd gotten my first driver's license, Jamie and I drove off to the pediatrician, whose office, in a new brick building, reminded me of a drive-through hamburger place. In all that well-lit cleanliness, sickness seemed so temporary, so easy to cure, and downright fun, and the pediatrician did little to dispel that notion. He seemed eight feet tall, and wore glasses-moustaches-noses, plastic boutonnieres, crazy hats, Groucho, Bozo, or Big Bird. His Donald Duck squawk made some kids laugh, and others run for cover. None of the mothers on our street liked him. He was loud, aggressive, and sometimes, terrifying.

"Can't climb onto the school bus?" he asked. It was a Bozo wig day. He called his colleague from across the hall. Whispering, they pushed at Jamie's arms, and legs, and I wished I could die right there, on the spot. The nurse came in and led Jamie outside. When the colleague left, and the doctor shut the door behind him, he took off the Bozo wig and reached for my hand, I wanted to run. The gig was up.

"We're going to take some blood," he said, his voice octaves lower and softer. "What do you think it could be?" I asked, all innocence, and hating myself. *Fine motor skills, I prayed. Something—anything—else.* I couldn't face this doctor and tell him about Richie. What would he think of me? "We'll get some blood," he said, letting go of my hand, and kneading the wig in his lap, "and we'll go from there." I considered grabbing the wig, putting it on, running out the door. Maybe that would've eliminated what came next. But what came next, a week after Jamie's seventh birthday, was a trip to the lab. I was a brand-new driver behind the wheel of a very old car that stalled, and there was Jamie, in his new Steelers football jersey, his new Sears "Toughskin" jeans that, as it turned out, he didn't need at all. "After the blood test," I told Jamie, "we'll stop at 7-Eleven and get some chocolate milk." "Yay!" Jamie said, blue eyes bright, his small fingers all scrunched together in his lap. *It's so easy to please him,* I thought, wondering idly how hard it would be to steer off the road and into a tree. It would make sense. I was such a new driver, after all. I couldn't stand thinking of how much unhappiness I was about to bring to all of them. Jamie most of all, but also to Patrick Jr., and Patrick Sr., who didn't have to know any of this, if only he'd married someone else.

When the doctor called with the results, his somber voice completely erased my memory of his outstanding Donald Duck. Jamie's CPK count was "astronomical." He'd arranged for us to see Dr. Alfred Spiro, a pediatric neurologist at Einstein

Hospital in the Bronx. In my mind's eye, I saw my mother's desperate, panicky look as the ramp lowered, and she and Richie were home from the clinic. *My God*, I thought, *how will we ever get through this?*

I'm sorry, sorry, sorry.

CHAPTER FIFTEEN

ON OCTOBER 16, 1980, ANOTHER BRILLIANT FALL DAY, the four of us were in the ancient red Toyota, on our way to see Dr. Spiro, at Einstein Hospital, in the Bronx. Before we left Suffolk County, Patrick got so violently sick to his stomach, that we had to get off the expressway and find a rest room.

Oh Patrick, I'm so sorry.

Other than Patrick's sick face, and the sudden stop, we thought we were hiding the seriousness of our trip from the boys, and it seemed to work. We're Irish, after all, and the laugh always has to be tucked in somewhere, like a handkerchief. Patrick slipped me the mickey, and I slipped it to him, and Patrick and Jamie slipped it to each other. This is how Patrick and I were raised—this is how we raised the boys. By the time we crossed the Throgs Neck Bridge, we were all downright giddy. Though Jamie was too tall, Patrick Sr. carried him piggyback through the pleasant streets and Patrick Jr. and I, holding hands, had to run to keep up with them. We skipped over the tree roots pushing their way through the sidewalk, and when we got to the doctor's office, on the third floor of the Rousso Building, the four of us were shown into the examining room, where we watched Jamie undress. We're tall, broad people, and Jamie was so slim. From across the chilly room, he seemed so slight. When I looked at him, under those fluorescent lights, it was 1966, and he was Richie all over again, right across the room from my mother and me in the neurology clinic of Elmhurst General Hospital. My mother and I didn't joke then, but fourteen years later, waiting for the doctor, we're full of laughs. A terrible compulsion, like being tickled to death.

Dr. Spiro watched Jamie walk cross the room, and I watched Dr. Spiro, but his face was impassive. He walked with Jamie through the door, and out to a staircase at the end of the hall, and watched him climb a small flight of stairs. When they came back, Dr. Spiro sat Jamie on the side of the examining table. Standing in front of Jamie, he picked up the rubber mallet, checked reflexes in Jamie's arms, knees, ankles. Then he put the mallet down on the crinkly white paper, and sat on a small stool in front of him. But then Jamie, who misunderstood our desperate hilarity, grabbed the mallet, and as if we were at the circus, bopped Dr. Spiro squarely on the top of his head, and laughed. We were mortified. We'd never seen Jamie do anything like that before. He wasn't that kind of kid. "Oh, that's okay," Dr. Spiro said, as if he'd been bopped a thousand times before.

But then there was a group of young doctors in the room, serious young men wearing yarmulkes, holding clipboards. They asked about our families. Any diseases? "My uncles were diagnosed with 'muscular apathy,'" I said. "They died in 1922." At the time, it was as much of a clue as I could admit to. I planned to tell them about Richie, but first, I wanted them to rule out everything else. They crowded around Jamie like elders in the temple, speaking to each other, in Latin, out of the sides of their mouths. They pointed to Jamie's legs, and we didn't know what they were pointing at. They were just Jamie's legs, and if you asked me, his muscles weren't even all that big. Before they left, they asked to see my legs too, and I thought of that ancient Jewish prayer thanking God for not being born a woman. Being born a woman was what probably saved my life.

A muscle biopsy was the next step, Dr. Spiro told us, necessary no matter what the family history. He said that they just needed "a small bit" of muscle from Jamie's thigh, a procedure more "uncomfortable" than painful, and an overnight stay in the hospital. Then they'd have a "definitive diagnosis." "As soon as possible," he urged, "so we know exactly what we're dealing with." We already had a pretty good idea of what we were dealing with—but we didn't tell Dr. Spiro that. He told us to call in a few days and schedule the biopsy. "But we don't know anything for sure," Patrick cautioned me, opening the car door, and helping Jamie into the seat, saying nothing all the way home. But when we got there, I found Patrick in the bedroom, just standing in front of his dresser. "What will we tell my parents?" I asked, for he'd already said he didn't want to tell his mother anything until we knew for sure. "We tell them *nothing* yet!" he said, slamming his top drawer, stalking out of the room.

"Even if it *is* dystrophy," my mother said, leaving the "muscular" out of the name—for after all, we're old friends, and why give the beast one more word, one more bit of unnecessary breath?—"they'll have treatment, they'll have a cure before Jamie ever sees a wheelchair." I tried to listen to the same old dusty speech, for my mother had just buried Richie, and she was trying so hard—unlike my father, the realist, who said nothing. When my mother-in-law called, and asked how things were, I said "Fine," although my cheeks hurt keeping this awful secret. Instead of telling her the truth—for after all, she lived only a few miles away from Einstein Hospital, and what if we somehow met her on the street?—I told my sister-in-law, Elizabeth, and swore her to secrecy. I needed a "beard," and she was it. Things weren't "fine" at all. I was convinced then that things would never be "fine" again.

Two or three times a week, Rose, Dr. Spiro's secretary, called, asking if we were ready to schedule the biopsy, yet for the longest time, we weren't ready. I could hardly get out of bed, and Patrick didn't want Jamie to have the biopsy at all. "It's just a minor procedure," I said, "and eventually it may help him," but Patrick was adamant. "Tell them about Richie," he said, "and maybe that'll be enough. I don't want him hurt any more than necessary." "They say it *is* necessary," I insisted, "even if there is a family history!" After two months of arguing, we came to a compromise. If I wanted the biopsy done, I'd be the one to take him. "It's only a small procedure," I said, but Patrick said he couldn't bear it. "Jamie needs a muscle biopsy," I told my parents, who stared at me and said nothing.

Richie was only gone a little more than a year. It was December by the time the biopsy was finally scheduled, and it was my father, who put on his tweed cap, and once again, stepped up to the plate. On a bright, frigid day, with Mom sitting next to him, Dad drove from Queens to Long Island to pick us up, and brought us to Einstein Hospital, where we waited in the sunny, chilly lobby for Jamie's name to be called. With Spiderman sneakers on his feet, and his auburn hair in his eyes, Jamie pranced around the lobby, trying to get Patrick Jr. to stroll around with him—but Patrick Jr. wouldn't leave my side. Eventually, of course, he left with my parents, looking back at me as they ushered him through the revolving door.

Jamie, who'd never been in a hospital before, was overjoyed with the phone right next to his bed, and the small, movable television right above his head. He climbed in and out of the bed, fussed with the TV, played with the phone, walked in and out of the bathroom. He didn't want to get undressed—I'm not sick! he insisted—and so I let him stay in his jeans. In the next bed was a boy of about twelve who had a brain tumor, and a shunt in his head. His beautifully dressed mother, father, and sister sat at a card table in front of his bed, and opened their Big Macs as if they were eating steak at Le Cirque. His mother told me he'd been in the hospital for a month. She smiled at Jamie, wondering, no doubt, what could be wrong with such a glowing child, but I didn't tell her. "He's here for some tests" is all I admitted to. In a weird terrible way, I envied her. Unlike DMD, cancer isn't necessarily hereditary. The cancer mother scared me, for I thought that this was it for us now, we were in the land of terribly sick children, and stalwart parents, and I wasn't stalwart. At bedtime, the other mother came out of the bathroom, like a Mother's Day ad, in a matching nightgown and robe, her blond hair loose around her shoulders. There were no Mother's Day ads for mothers dressed like me. At home, I slept in one of Patrick's T-shirts and an old half-slip. They weren't going to get *me* to settle in—both Jamie and I would stay in our clothes, thank you very much. I didn't think I was neat enough, pleasant enough, certainly not blond enough, to see Jamie through this. I didn't think I could bear to see him disintegrate like Richie did. I didn't want to wear my mother's orthopedic shoes, or live her terribly hard housework, cooking, laundry life. Just when I decided to take Jamie home, not put him through more when I knew already what was wrong, thinking Patrick had been right, and the hell with it, there *still* wasn't any treatment, Elizabeth came into the room, and she'd brought old Father Duffy, a Franciscan priest and family friend, along with her, and he was in full regalia. A robe, a hood, and even though it was freezing outside, sandals on his bare feet. I'd heard a clicking noise in the hall outside that I realized were Father Duffy's rosary beads brushing against the wall. A priest in full habit, especially on the pediatric floor, especially in a room where there is a very sick child, attracts quite a crowd. There were half a dozen nurses standing in the doorway, but old Father Duffy was oblivious, sailing past Jamie, and heading straight toward the card table, a priest on a mission. With their mouths full, terrified, the boy's family looked up from their Cokes. The blond father, in his pin-striped navy suit, tried to scramble to his feet but all the Latin had him confused. Father Duffy blessed the boy, the blond mother, who looked a little like Pat Nixon in her green dress, the blond father and the sister too, his old, wrinkly, liver-spotted hands resting on her blond curls. I closed my eyes, and prayed to God that they were at least *Catholics*.

At dawn, they put Jamie into a hospital gown, and gave him a shot, but it didn't seem to work. He was completely alert, and beginning to whimper, even when the orderly picked him up in his arms, put him on the gurney, and rolled him directly across the hall to the "treatment room." I was the one who felt woozy, walking down the corridor to the leather couch in front of the elevators to wait, where I first heard the screams, and for a minute, I couldn't imagine where they could be coming from. It can't be Jamie, I thought—Dr. Spiro said that the procedure wasn't painful, only "a little uncomfortable." I'd never heard screams like that from any little kid. Curious, I got up, and walked back toward Jamie's room, when I realized, with a growing horror, that it was Jamie, and he was screaming for me. Pushing through the "treatment room" door, I saw him, on the table, writhing and kicking, and he was in agony. Wearing a mask, a cap, and a blood-spotted apron, Dr. Spiro whirled around to face me. He said that Jamie was doing well, that the procedure was almost over, and then someone was pushing me back through the door, and out into the hall-way, where there was nothing to do but wait. And cry. And try to hide my face from the maintenance man, who stared at me while he polished the floor.

When the "minor procedure" was over, and Jamie was back in his room, they couldn't wake him. Later, they'd tell me that kids with MD sometimes have an odd reaction to anesthesia, but nobody told me that then. The nurses couldn't wake him. I couldn't wake him. He slept, and slept. I ran to the phone in the hall and in tears, called Patrick—who never said "I told you so" but got into the car, and less than an hour later was standing at Jamie's bedside, spooning vanilla ice cream into his mouth. When the three of us got back to Mom and Dad's apartment, it seemed almost funny to me to see that Mom had a big roast leg of lamb in the oven, the exact same meal we had on the hot day Richie was diagnosed. Why not, for once in our lives, ham and cheese sandwiches on paper plates with a big bag of chips, and a jug of mustard on the table instead of the brimming gravy boat? A thrown-together dinner on Mom's gleaming table would have surprised me no more than the Rockettes kicking their way out of her tiny bathroom. But maybe Mom knew what she was doing. Only a few hours from the dead sleep of anesthesia, Jamie ate a huge dinner, and slept all the way home.

It's confirmed. The bitch was back and the geneticist wanted to meet with us. We're not to give up hope, Dr. Spiro said. Modern medicine, amazing strides all the time. Physical therapy helped. Did we want Jamie to be evaluated, and see the physical therapist? Yes, of course. We wanted to do anything we could. Something was better than nothing. At first, we didn't realize that there was no way we could come from Eastern Long Island to the Bronx, twice a week. I hadn't yet driven on any major roads, Patrick had a demanding job, the boys were in school. We trudged off to the physical therapy room anyway, where there were a lot of mirrors, a long barre, like a ballet school, to wait for the evaluating physician. Patrick and Pat wandered off in search of a cool drink when the doctor came into the room. She was a heavy woman in her late fifties with a thick foreign accent. She was the first to ask the questions I would answer for the next seventeen years. Full-term baby, no problems during pregnancy or birth. Excellent Apgar. "My older son is normal," I said, and she looked at me. The one thing I was holding onto in that place of abnormality was my normal older son. He was handsome, smart, popular, healthy, so very "right," the "rightest" thing that had ever happened to me. In my heart, I knew I didn't deserve a son like that, and if truth be told, I was always waiting for him to be snatched away. The doctor asked to see me outside. I followed her, and in the corridor, safely out of Jamie's sight, she put her thick hands on my shoulders and looked deep into my eyes. "Don't ever say that one son is 'normal,'" she said. "This son is not 'abnormal,'" and no, no, that is not what I meant, not at all, and I clung to her and cried. Richie's life—my mother's life—was not what I wanted for Jamie, and me. They were a lot tougher than we were.

"I can't do this," I murmured into the doctor's strong neck, and though I wanted to say "again" I didn't. I had no idea then that like every other "special" parent, I was well-prepared, and that raising a handicapped child is a little like being asked to go camping, and finding in the back of the hall closet, a Coleman lantern, a tent, the Swiss Army Knife you never knew you had. I never suspected that there would be kind of a map, with so many sparks to follow, that for seventeen of Jamie's twenty-four years, it would be like being at the beach, and looking up at the starry night sky. Dr. Spiro had said that Jamie would live to be "at least" sixteen. They'd said that Richie would live to be twelve—and yet he had ten more years. "Sure you can," the doctor said, but I shook my head. My nose was dripping onto her white coat. She pushed my hair away from my forehead, handed me a tissue, grabbed my wrist, and led me back into the room.

Patrick didn't want to see the geneticist. "What's the point?" he asked. "We don't want any more kids." He said he was sick of these people, sick of the hospital, sick of the whole stinking thing. "No matter what they do," he said, "they can't cure Jamie." He said he just wanted to take Pat and Jamie home, let them play with their friends, have dinner, buy them an ice cream. He said we'd all been through enough, and it had only just begun. "Go and see the geneticist," he said, "I'll take the kids and wait downstairs." As soon as I sat down, I regretted it. She had the results of the biopsy, and Jamie was burning a gazillion muscles a day. "I *have* to tell you this," she said. "Why?" I wanted to ask. There's nothing they can do, and every night when I put him to bed, it'll make me feel terrible. A gazillion more muscles. "You should think about having more children," she said, eager for me to replace the doomed child I had, "you're only thirty years old." She told me that prenatal testing to determine the baby's sex could now be done in the first few months (rather than waiting for the fifth-month amnio), and if it's another male, then "we" can abort. In 1980, it would be a while before they'd know any sooner if a male fetus was healthy or not. Only I can't abort, for even thinking about it breaks my heart. And even if I were to conceive a girl, I ask her, how can I give Jamie what he is going to need? And what about Patrick Jr.? And what would happen when this possible daughter wanted to have children of her own? Suppose they never cure it? I knew muscular dystrophy better than the geneticist did. I didn't want to take anything else away from the children I already had—though if I had done so, Patrick now might have a sibling. Still, in 1980, another pregnancy wasn't the right decision for me, for us.

That night, when we were back on Long Island, and the boys were safely asleep, I found Patrick in the bedroom again, sitting on the side of the bed, clutching a pillow to his chest, weeping torrents of tears. *"What have we done to him, what have we done to him?"* he sobbed. There's nothing I could do but sit next to him, wrap my arms around his waist, hold on tight. For six months, I'd hear him crying in his sleep. The next morning, we told Jamie and Patrick that Jamie's leg muscles were weak, and that's why he was falling, and that's why he was having such a hard time with the stairs, and it wasn't his fault. "Is Jamie handicapped?" Patrick asked, and Jamie said, "I'm footicapped!" and despite myself, I smiled.

There was the school principal to tell, the bearlike Mr. Myer, who hired Mrs. Lynch, a kindhearted, gentle mother of four, to be Jamie's aide in school, and arranged for Jamie to have after-school swim lessons at the high school pool. Another spark, another light to follow. Then there were the school social workers, the religious education office at church, where Jamie's class met in a basement room. A relief to legitimately, openly carry Jamie up and down the stairs, a thousand pounds lifted at once. The neighbors all knew. "I thought it was peculiar that he had such a hard time getting up from the ground," one of the neighbors said, and I said, "That's called a Gower's Maneuver" in what sounded to me like Walter Cronkite's voice, as if we were talking about some kid in the newspaper, and not Jamie—although Walter Cronkite, a professional person who didn't wear his heart on his sleeve, had lessons to teach me if I wanted to get through this thing. Even if I stood on my head and spit nickels, as my mother said, we were going to lose Jamie, and I'd better get used to the idea. My Walter Cronkite resolve lasted about a minute before I wondered where I was when this neighbor was watching Jamie get up from the ground, and how I could shield him from a future in a wheelchair, and all those staring eyes.

On Christmas night, I knelt on the living-room rug in front of my mother-in-law, like the penitent I felt myself to be, and I took her hand, crying and apologizing all over the place, and finally told her that Jamie has DMD. She was shocked, and in the beginning, furious with all of us, including her own daughter, who'd kept this awful secret from her, but she was a flash-angry person who got over things as quickly as they came on, a simple woman with a strong faith I sometimes envied. "Whatever God wants," she said, and though the idea of God wanting muscular dystrophy to take another innocent boy made me want to punch God's face, it was a profound thought in three small words, and from time to time over the next seventeen years would give me more solace than I'd ever have believed.

Because my own family had been so decimated by muscular dystrophy, in a sort of medical catch-22, I had hardly any relatives to tell about Jamie, and muscular dystrophy. The relatives I had to tell were Patrick's—and I dreaded it. Educated, successful, charming, polite, Patrick's relatives are the nicest people in the world, and here I was, dragging this awful thing into their midst. That our son's illness would impact them only minimally, if at all, did not yet occur to me. It was terrible, and it was my fault. If they'd wanted to stone me, I'd have gladly agreed. They were the relatives of my dreams, this Irish/Italian family that I was enthralled to be only the smallest part of. They were better than any of the cake-carrying relatives I so envied when I was a kid. Politics, religion, books, are what they discussed, and Patrick following them from one subject to the next gave me not only goose bumps but an education. I didn't know half of what they did, and yet I did my part, laboring over the thank-you notes, sending little notes tucked inside the Christmas cards, and I was always prompt with the RSVP. I was ever on the alert for pertinent magazine or newspaper clippings. I desperately wanted Patrick's fine family to like me. I wanted them to know that Jamie's sickness was completely my fault, my failing, my sin. Mixed up as it now sounds, I didn't want Patrick's relatives to think any less of him—but Patrick flat-out refused to make any big announcement. "Now that my mother knows," he said, "everyone else will too. It doesn't have to be such a big deal," but this was not good enough for me, and so, at a family picnic, with Elizabeth at my side, I cornered Cousin Frank, who was in the kitchen just looking for some ice. It seemed only right to begin with Frank, for not only was he Jamie's godfather, but he is such a kind man. I was shaking so much that I had to hold Elizabeth's hand, so emotional and raw that Cousin Joe, Frank's younger brother, had to turn and leave the room. They are such good people that they deserved to hear this news from me, straight from the horse's mouth, and if Patrick wouldn't tell them, then I thought I had to. It was my fault, my job. Poor Frank—he didn't know what to say. He asked about treatments, about research, nodding politely at everything I said while Patrick and the kids were in the yard eating hamburgers and hotdogs.

We agreed with Mr. Meyer, the Waverly School principal that Jamie should take the regular school bus as long as he "comfortably" could, and so in the mornings, after I walked with Patrick and Jamie to the school bus, I came home, and went back to bed, rousing myself only when the school bus was due. If I got up to go to the bathroom, or make a cup of tea, I walked through the silent rooms to see what it would be like when he was gone. I had my driver's license, finally, and on good days, I left my bed and drove to the kids' school, where they took pity on me, and let me stand in the hallway, and look into his classroom. It was terrible if he fell while I was standing there. He didn't know I was watching, and he looked so perplexed. I saw his teacher pick him up as quickly as she could, and when he came home, I reassured him that falling wasn't his fault; I reminded him that his muscles weren't strong. We told him that the doctors were working hard to find medicine for boys with MD, and he was satisfied. He nodded, I washed his face, and he was off, walking on his toes, with his belly sticking out, making his precarious way to his bedroom, or to the kitchen, onto the next thing. "What is, is," the adult Jamie often said, and then went back to his crossword puzzle. Despite all he'd lost, I never saw Jamie cry. Thick as mud, Jamie was stubborn and tough. Strangely enough, Patrick was the one I worried about, his feelings all over his beautiful face.

At night, after I took the garbage out, I stood on the porch, in the dark, looking through the window, through the organdy curtains, at the short shelf life of my sons tussling together on the red rug, at Patrick Jr., so big and strong, so careful not to hurt a brother so much weaker and smaller, yet so safe underneath him. It's a memory I've preserved under glass. It was Patrick Jr. who remembered Richie's all too recent struggle, Patrick Jr. who seemed to hurt more. At night, when Patrick Sr. was working late, or off on a business trip, when the boys were sitting at the kitchen table doing homework, and I was sitting across from them reading the newspaper, they told me what they wanted to be when they grow up. "I'm gonna be a doctor," Patrick said, "and cure diseases." "I'm gonna be an Air Force fighter pilot," Jamie said while Patrick stared at me.

When Patrick Sr. was home, he was appalled at the state of the house, the quality of the meals, the piles of laundry. He couldn't understand why the T-shirts in the bottom of the laundry basket were growing moldy, why we had hardly any groceries, why our bed was never made—but he was so seldom home, that he didn't know how much time I spent there. He didn't know that I spent most of my time crying. I cried when I looked at Patrick and Jamie playing together—in spite of what I thought of as Jamie's "death sentence," they were so innocent, and they seemed so happy. I cried when I thought of Richie. I cried when I thought of the wheelchairs that were on their way to us. I even cried for my poor hair, springy and curly, wanting so hard to live while the rest of me wanted to die. When I dragged myself out to dinner one Saturday night with Patrick and his coworkers, who knew nothing about Jamie, muscular dystrophy was all I could talk about. We left early and fought all the way home. He felt the same way I did, the exact same way, but he had to go to work and be with people in the world anyway. If he were to "wallow" like I was doing, none of us would survive. "That's true," I said, "but you didn't cause it." "You didn't cause it either, for Christ's sake!" he yelled. "We *both* caused it . . . Why can't you understand that?" he asked, changing lanes, roaring along the highway while I looked out the window, and cried some more.

Then one day my mother called and told me, for Christ's sake, to get up out of that goddamn bed, that enough is enough, that the kids needed their mother, and that Patrick needed a wife, and she didn't raise a quitter. "You're falling down on the job," she said, and I realized that she was right. If only I'd known then that anything can be endured in tiny bits, or that one pair of hands would always be there to hand us over to another—how much easier it would have seemed. Half-crazy though I was, when I got up, I knew that to survive,

I had to develop a hide, a thickness, a coat—in those Reagan years, something like a Star Wars shield—and be somebody completely different.

The first MDA Support Group Meeting I went to was informal, in Noranne Hill's house in Ronkonkoma, a few miles away. The Muscular Dystrophy Association had given me Noranne's name and telephone number. When I called to introduce myself, Noranne told me that she also had a brother with DMD. Her sixteen-year-old son Matthew had DMD, and so did her youngest, four-year-old Patrick. When I got to her house to meet the other support group members, I came through the door, and immediately had to jump out of the way, for Matthew was flying past in his motorized wheelchair, on his way to the den, which was filled with boys watching basketball. There was loud teenage music playing, and the dining-room table was full of cold cuts for whoever was hungry. It could be a Saturday afternoon in a million other American homes. In Noranne's house, people had to eat, the laundry had to be done, and DMD was just another circumstance. DMD didn't stop Noranne and her husband Jack from taking in an orphaned foster child who also had DMD, from taking in a young Catholic girl who was pregnant and had nowhere to go, and from taking Jack's aged mother to live with them. Most surprising of all is when Noranne told me that Patrick, her DMD brother, lived into his mid-thirties. "Into his *thirties*?" I asked. "Well, he smoked," Noranne said, and we both laughed. "Don't you feel so guilty passing it on?" I asked her, though we'd just met. "No," Noranne said, "I just figure it was

God's will." Oh, how I wished I could figure that too. "Jamie's doctor said he'd live to be sixteen," I said. "Oh, they always tell you that," she said, and for the first time, I felt the tiniest dollop of hope. Thirty—that would give Jamie another twenty-three years, and in twenty-three years, well, everything could change. It was in Noranne's living room, watching all the activity around me, that I learn to fit this fatal illness into our everyday life on our terms—wearing it, softening it, molding it, so that it fits us rather than the other way around. It was in Noranne's living room that I got Jamie back, the Jamie he was before the diagnosis, the Jamie he'd been all along.

CHAPTER SIXTEEN

USCULAR APATHY, MUSCULAR SCLEROSIS, MULTI-ple apathy, multiple dystrophy—nobody ever got the name of the goddamn thing right, not even the doctors. One doctor asked me if I knew that "multiple dystrophy" was hereditary, and did I plan on having any more children? "Not if they turn out to be doctors," I said. "How is his mind?" strangers asked, right in front of Jamie, as if he weren't there, the same question—they even looked like the same strangers—they'd asked right in front of Richie. "He's off his rocker" was what Richie said in 1975. Ten years later, Jamie said, "He's out to lunch."

"You know, the Jerry Lewis Telethon?" was what I must have asked a hundred people who wanted to know what was wrong with Jamie. (When Chris and Jason were diagnosed, however, the nonexistent, imaginary, all-in-the-head "multiple dystrophy" was exactly right.) Appropriately enough, it was on a Good Friday that Jamie's first wheelchair, a tiny black-and-royal-blue "Quickie" (which was a bit like calling someone with an artificial leg "Flash") was delivered, wrapped in plastic like a caul. When the deliveryman left, the furniture hugged the walls, and the living room was Dodge City quiet—but I'd already decided that on the inevitable day when the wheelchair showed up, I'd accept it. There would be no shoot out over some black cushions, some Velcro straps, a small steel base. The whole thing was nothing more than a help to Jamie. Nothing to panic over. It wasn't Richie's wheelchair—it wasn't Richie's MD. Maybe our story would have a different ending. Who's to say? It really didn't look much different to me than one of those futuristic chairs in the *New York Times*. It didn't seem half as out of place to me as Richie's wheelchair had, for we were in suburbia, and everyone rolls through suburban life on wheels.

"Hey God," I asked the empty living room, while Finny, our homely beagle, stared at me. "How hard is it to assemble children with parts that work?"

But then, before I knew it, we were all relieved that Jamie wouldn't fall any more—that is, until he went over the "jump ramp" and split his lip—and it was Chris Diaz, instead of Danny O'Rourke, riding on the back with his arms wrapped around Jamie's neck, and Jamie instead of Richie, laughing his head off, with the wind blowing through his hair.

"What can't be cured," my mother said, "must be endured."

What is, is.

When we brought Patrick Jr. to the Stony Brook emergency room with an eye infection, a nurse told Jamie to "get out of that wheelchair," and "stop playing around." Astonished, the four of us looked at each other and laughed. "But I don't think of myself as handicapped," Jamie said later on, in the parking lot, when Patrick Sr. took him out of the wheelchair, and plopped him into the backseat, right next to Patrick Jr., whose sore eye was covered by a big white patch. "Good for you," Patrick Sr. said, rubbing Jamie's head. Patrick Jr., turning his head to look at Jamie with his good eye, smiled at his brother. If Patrick developed a sore throat, a fever, a cough, he knew that the first order of business was staying away from Jamie. Whenever he felt a cold coming on, it was Patrick Jr. who frantically searched for the Lysol spray, and voluntarily sequestered himself in his bedroom. Whenever any of us had a cold, it was Patrick Jr., age nine, ten, eleven, who instantly went looking for Jamie's toothbrush, and stuck it on a high shelf in the linen closet, far away from the others. After Christopher's spinal fusion, when his lung collapsed, and he was airlifted, in the middle of the night, to Hartford Hospital, it was Patrick Jr. who drove four hours to get to him. Anything other than muscular dystrophy—which was in our homes, our kitchens, our beds, underneath the doors and windows of our life on Long Island, and my sister's life in Connecticut, like the old movie, *The Blob*—can be endured. Pam and I worked hard at making home, with its pretty curtains, its clean sheets, its full refrigerator, its shiny kitchen floor, "the best," whether we wanted to be there or not. It is no small thing to come home at night to a hot meal, and someone who loves you. Chris and Jason were part of a research group, and Pam and Charlie took them, by plane, back and forth to Rochester, New York. Despite his critics, Jerry Lewis and the Muscular Dystrophy Association offered us the best doctors, the best clinics, the best services, and I will always be grateful for his efforts. Every other month, Jamie had an appointment with Dr. Spiro, and in the meantime, in school, there were Committee on the Handicapped Meetings, physical therapy sessions, swimming. I wrote to radio nutritionist Carlton Fredericks, who wrote back, and sent us to a nutritionist in Red Hook, New Jersey for some dietary advice. Pam and I were on the phone all the time, up to our elbows in selenium, and vitamin E, in wheat germ and soy milk and broccoli that none of the boys would eat, and then we were back to the normal foods on our "fine Irish tables," including the occasional Ring Ding. There were adaptive gym classes for Jamie, who locked the adaptive gym teacher in the volleyball closet—we couldn't believe this either, for he still wasn't that kind of kid—and then the handicapped bus had to wait for him outside the detention classroom.

We found ourselves with everything we needed to get by.

My father died before all three of the boys went into those Fisher-Price–size wheelchairs, and it was my mother, by herself, who gave away the cream-and-white carpeting, the coffee table, the round tables with the Irish lace tablecloths to make way for the wheelchairs that had come back in her life. Her brothers, her cousins, her son, her grandsons. Just when you thought it was safe. We couldn't believe that this had happened again, and again, and again. When Jamie told me I was beautiful, "like Christie Brinkley, Mom, and isn't it funny that you both have almost the same name?" and that I was "kind, like the Blessed Mother," that he thought I was his "guardian angel," and that the prayers he knew I said for him were what kept him "strong," I pulled down the Star Wars shield, and gave him a big hug. "Of course," I said, clearing my throat of the catch in it when he asked if he could kick when he was inside of me. When he asked me what it felt like to run, I scooped him out of the wheelchair, and with Jamie in my arms, and bladder control a risky issue, I ran through the house. We bought a sled, and on the first big snowstorm of that first wheelchair year, I ran down the street pulling him behind me. He was so light, I thought, my lungs full of crispy, cold air, and my mind filled with thoughts of the life that mattered. It wasn't until I was almost home that I realized that the sled was empty, and Jamie was halfway down the block, face-down in a snowdrift. I could see his sneakers sticking out of the snow—something he couldn't resist reminding me of years later, when his wheelchair flipped over inside the van, on the Southern State Parkway, on our way to get his back brace made, while I was not paying much attention to the bend in the road, and was singing my heart out to "Me and Bobby McGee."

When Jamie needed wheelchair fittings, or repairs, I let him take half the neighborhood to the surgical store with us, and looked the other way when half a dozen little boys squeezed the breast protheses and peered into the incontinence briefs the dummies wore, and then we went to McDonald's. As a healer, daily-ness is underestimated. Pam and Charlie, Patrick and I bought vans, and we girls learned to drive them, and almost immediately, a block away from home, I hit the angry

Doberman belonging to the neighborhood crazy people, whose front lawn was suspiciously covered with gnomes. After I hit that dog, he was never the same. He wouldn't leave the lawn, a canine Gulliver in a town of gnome Lilliputians—but the neighborhood became a lot safer. It's all in how you look at it.

Though Dad was gone, the thought of his seeing either of us behind the wheels of our huge vehicles made Pam and me laugh. He hadn't thought either one of us was any good at driving anything. He liked to remind me that until I was twelve, my bike had training wheels. "What are you gonna do if that guy stops suddenly?" he'd ask, from the passenger seat, poking Pam or me in the right shoulder. When I was eighteen, he'd tried to teach me to drive, and just as I was about to hit the double-parked police car, he bent down and pressed on my foot, which was on the brake, with both hands.

Pam and I decided that we weren't about to let a little thing like three boys with muscular dystrophy get in the way of a family vacation, and so for a week in the summer of 1985, Pam and Charlie, Patrick and I, and all the boys rented adjoining cabins in Lake George, New York. Jamie was in the Quickie full-time, Chris was in his Quickie part-time, and Jason was a "slow-ie" in leg braces. It took us a long time to get anywhere, and we weren't yet accustomed to so many staring crowds, all of the vacationers staring at us with squinty eyes, trying to figure out what exactly was wrong, if we were a family, or a school, and so therefore, we moved through the amusement parks, and the water ride parks, and the general points of interest as quietly and as invisibly as a mess of wheelchairs and leg braces would allow, and in this way, we rode a paddle boat, played arcade games, ate more greasy meals than we should have, and coincidentally, brought home with us generations of mice who seemed to be on a vacation of their own, traveling in our suitcases along with our dirty clothes.

We saved the Revolutionary War reenactment for the last day, and because it took us so long to go anywhere, we were late, and crowds were already seated on folding chairs in the center of Fort Henry, leaning, with rapt attention, on their knees. We were halfway up the narrow side ramp—pushing wheelchairs, pulling Jason—when suddenly one hundred musket-carrying Redcoats, moonlighting cashiers, or ice cream fillers at Dairy Queen, were bearing down on us. One of the Redcoats tripped over Jamie's chair, and fell on his knees. "Yonder!" the narrator yelled, pointing straight at us, and four thousand Lake George vacationers in baggy shorts stood up, craned their necks, confused. Were these the wounded soldiers? Were we part of the show?

We weren't quite sure ourselves.

CHAPTER SEVENTEEN

O N THE MORNING OF MAY 20, 1970, THIRTY MIN-utes after Pam had left for high school, while Mom was standing at the sink, and Richie and I were sit-ting at the table eating cereal, we heard on the radio that there had been a terrible subway crash—with fatalities—at the Seventy-fourth Street, Jackson Heights station. It was a beau-tiful spring day, twenty-eight years to the beautiful spring day that my as-yet-unborn son Jamie would die, and a month to the day before Patrick's and my wedding. The three of us stared at each other. Then Mom ran to the coat closet in the hall and threw her raincoat over her nightgown, pulled on her shoes, ran out of the apartment and headed for the subway. Five minutes after she left, Pam called. She'd gotten the earlier train. "Go tell Mom," Richie said, "I'll be fine," and though we never left him alone in the apartment, I ran out the door, and along Roosevelt Avenue until I found my mother. She was ashen-faced, leaning against the plate-glass window of an up-holstery shop, as if she couldn't stand up under her own speed.

Later, she would tell me that she had seen Catholic schoolkids in uniforms just like Pam's being carried out of the station on stretchers. When she saw me crossing the street, running toward her, not knowing what I was about to tell her, her nervous system went berserk, and she fainted. Right onto the sidewalk. An old man passing by helped me pull her to her feet. It frightened me. Until that moment, I'd never imagined the depth of a mother's love. Years later, when I was a mother myself, and read the Edna O'Brien short story about a mother who wants to be buried with her child, and says that the only true love there is exists between mother and child, I thought of that spring day, and I understood.

Only because my grandmother, Sadie, had lived into her eighties, did I think my mother would too. After all, Mom had always seemed so much younger than her own mother. At sixty, Nana was wearing orthopedic shoes, house dresses, corsets. She sighed almost all the time, and wore her gray hair in a long silver braid wrapped tightly around her head. When Mom was seventy-eight, she was a sneaker-and-blue-jeans strawberry blonde, a teetotaler, with a barfly's ambience. Nana called us "Chicken," but Mom called everyone "Babe," or "Dear Heart." Nana was agoraphobic, but Mom loved the city. Nana was always gloomy, and "ailing" (according to Mom, Nana had "enjoyed ill health all of her life"), but Mom, in a sporadically kept journal we'd found after her death, admitted that she'd "never relinquished my girlhood dreams." Nana always said she was "heading for the last roundup," but Mom was heading for Bloomingdale's. Nana didn't give a fig about any of the neighbors, but Mom was her own apartment house Internet. "Inguinal hernia, prolapsed uterus," she'd said of one startled-looking old couple we'd met coming out of the elevator. "Deviated septum, colostomy bag, cancer of the throat" was how she described her neighbors, everyone in Mom's building reduced to baggy clothes full of bad parts. Until Mom's last few months when the "arthritis" in her left leg proved to be an undiagnosed blockage, she was always well.

Nana never read a thing, not even the newspaper, but Mom read three newspapers a day, and was seldom without a book in her hands. Unlike Mom, Nana wouldn't have known James Thurber, or Dorothy Parker, two of my mother's literary heroes, if they'd fallen on her head. It was Thurber when I called her in the morning ("The fletchers are here with the reeves," is what Mom said into the telephone, rather than a simple "hello") and Parker when we met in person. "A girl's best friend is her mutter," she'd say, telling me to "speak up, girlie" rather than admit her hearing was going.

On May 25, 1997, on a rainy Sunday morning, just as I was about to drive Mom home after a weekend visit, Patrick and I heard a terrible crash in the kitchen, and found her, unconscious, in the fetal position, on the floor. Because the only blood I could see was a thin stream from her nose, I'd thought she'd simply slipped from the chair. "What fresh hell is *this*?" I expected her to sit up and ask, one of her favorite Parkerisms, but she was gone. With Patrick's hand on mine, we did the chest compressions the 911 operator led us through, and I did the mouth to mouth—but it was too late. There was no response. There was nothing for Patrick to do but hold her in his arms, and nothing for me to do but stroke her hair. "I love you, Mommy. I love you, Mommy" was what Patrick said I'd repeated, over and over again, and though Jamie agreed, I don't remember. Poor Jamie. Patrick Jr. had spent the night in the Hamptons with his friends, but Jamie was in bed, couldn't move, and didn't know what was going on. Afterward, he asked me who the little girl in the kitchen had been—that's how young he'd said I'd sounded. "What's wrong, Dad? What's wrong?" he'd cried but we were in such shock, that we couldn't answer him. When it was clear there was nothing more to do, Patrick left me in the kitchen, with my mother, and went to calm Jamie. Then the ambulance pulled up, the EMTs jumped out, so young they looked like trick-or-treaters, standing on the porch.

No ocean voyage, no foreign journey, no treacherous expedition seemed more difficult to me at that moment than getting up from the floor with the taste of my mother's blood in my mouth, and crossing that gray living-room carpeting to get to the front door and let them in. When they rolled the stretcher past me, I couldn't stop staring at her hands. I'd never seen them so relaxed. Her hands had always been clenched in anxious fists, the palms bright red and sore from her own fingernails, her nervous stigmata. I thought of the tangerine silk drapes she never finished sewing, how her hands had fussed with the buckram. I'd never seen her hands that idle, that finished, that complete. So much for the Cape Cod, eightieth-birthday weekend I thought that Pam, Mom, and I would have, when we'd sit on wicker chairs on the porch of some bed and breakfast, and tie up any "loose ends." It was too late for that. That Sunday morning, the simple act of looking away from my mother's face was the tiniest, most final, of good-byes.

A few weeks before, on the Saturday before Mother's Day, Mom and I had gone to Clark's on Eighty-second Street in Jackson Heights where my mother ordered her pink chiffon "grandmother of the groom" dress for Patrick's upcoming September wedding. "This is *your* dress, little girl," she'd said, pushing a two-piece beige silk dress with a brocade jacket into my arms. She was right—it fit like a dream. When I came out of the dressing room in the gown, and looked for Mom, she was sitting on a fussy little red velvet pincushion of a chair, right in the middle of the mirrors. She looked up at me—three mothers looking up at me, almost more than I could stand, and smiled. "You look like Grace Kelly," she said, looking tiny, pale, old, despite the hair, the bright lipstick. *Only a mother,* I thought, *could think a full-figured, six-feet-tall, middle-aged daughter looks like Grace Kelly.* Mom's blue eyes looked watery, and sad to me, her eyelids red-rimmed. I told myself that she might be having a bad day, but Irish mothers don't tell, and Irish daughters learn to look away, and not to ask. Dad had been gone thirteen years, and Richie for eighteen, yet neither Pam nor I had ever seen our mother shed a tear. Mom didn't like "criers," the ones who "wore their hearts on their sleeves." Her bad times she kept to herself. They were, as she called them, her "little red wagons." When she seemed to be a little down, I suggested she join Senior Citizens, a prayer group, a reading group at the library. Why didn't she volunteer at a soup kitchen? "A soup kitchen," she said, looking at me, wiggling her thinning eyebrows, "smelly old men. Lice." "How about church?" I asked. "Creeping Jesus holy rollers." "Well, why don't you join the agnostic church?" I asked her. She laughed. "Why don't you stick your suggestions up your arse?" was her rejoinder.

We left Clark's, and went to lunch at Jahns' Ice Cream Parlor. While we waited for our tuna fish sandwiches and our Cokes, a very old lady in a big hat passed our table, and dropped a twenty-dollar bill. I bent down, picked it up, followed the old lady to the back of the restaurant, and gave it to her. When I came back, and sat down, I was shocked to see, for the first time, that my mother was crying. "What's wrong?" I asked, alarmed. "You have no idea how much I love you," she said, putting her hand over mine. Her hand was small, and mine was big, yet they are the same square hands. "If anything ever happens to me," she said, for the first and only time, "I want you to know that you and I have had a perfect mother and daughter relationship." I was stunned. I didn't want to say anything. I didn't want to let her go. I squeezed her hand. "I love you too," I said, too overcome to say any more. Though she'd live only for a couple of weeks, I knew that we were saying good-bye. I was heartsick driving all the way home, and yet when I pulled into the driveway, I was greeted by an eight-feet-tall chicken Jamie had hired to deliver a "Happy Mother's Day" singing telegram—and I once again found the Star Wars shield and pulled it down tight.

Mom never got to be grandmother of the groom, but she got to wear the pink chiffon dress. At the funeral home, she was beautiful. She looked like a bakery confection, like a bright peony, like Grace Kelly herself. On the last night, when everyone had gone, and we were alone with her, Jamie asked his father to pick him up and carry him to the casket. He was in Patrick's arms when I guided his small, misshapen hand to her cheek. When you're in a wheelchair for all those years, almost all of the touching is done to you. Less than a year later, we'd be in that room for him.

Sobbing at the funeral, Patrick Jr. stood up and struggled through a poem by Mark Twain, written upon the death of his daughter:

> *Warm summer sun shine brightly here*
> *Warm summer wind blow softly here*
> *Green sod above*
> *Lie light, lie light*
> *Goodnight, dear heart*
> *Goodnight, goodnight*

"Good thing they didn't give you a long poem," Jamie said.

Back at the house, after almost everyone had left, and I was alone in the kitchen, a motherless daughter, not four feet away from where my mother had died, I glanced through the screen door to the deck, where Ruthie and her mother Bea, and Linda and her mother, Rhoda, were sitting at the table laughing.

Amazing, isn't it, how thoroughly a flimsy screen door can separate one world from another?

CHAPTER EIGHTEEN

I DON'T KNOW WHAT I'LL DO IF ANYTHING HAPPENS to you," I told Jamie some months before he died, a couple of pneumonias into the year. When he'd ask me how long I thought he would live, the same question that my brother had asked all those years before, I'd simply told him he wouldn't live to be old, that he shouldn't worry about how long but instead, how deep—advice I'd still give him today. But if I had to do it again, I wouldn't tell him to eat more, drink more, not give me such a hard time when I want to take him for a ride in the van. I'd force myself to see that he could barely breathe, barely swallow, could hardly sit upright without a series of belts blistering his chest. If I watched him gasping for air, what I secretly thought of as his "fish breathing," I wouldn't tell him to close his mouth and try to breathe through his nose. I'd accept that when he closed his mouth, he couldn't breathe at all. I wouldn't tell him that he should be more positive, more optimistic, that the Bible itself says that a cheerful spirit is good medicine. I wouldn't want "don't give up" to be my present-day message. It sounds too much like "don't dare die."

"You'll be alright," he said, staring into my eyes until I looked away, a conversation I remembered about a year later, on a Sunday afternoon, when Patrick called me into the living room to see a football play, and I came out of the bedroom to read him a poem. I hate football. He hates poetry. I don't know why it is that miracles come into our lives wearing toe shoes, yet the disasters show up in construction boots—but Jamie was right. We're alright.

But in Jamie's last year, that Sunday afternoon was still many miles away.

From nine to five on weekdays in Jamie's last year, his nurse Diane spent hours upon hours sitting in the rocking chair next to him, in front of the TV, or the Scrabble board, or the *Sunday Times* crossword puzzle propped up on Jamie's hospital tray. Diane came to nursing later in life, but she was a natural at it—optimistic, cheerful, and very, very smart. She knew when Jamie was sick—sicker than usual, anyway—and she knew when he was bluffing. While Diane was telling Jamie about her sons, her ex-husband, her boyfriend, her mother, her neighborhood, an encounter with a surly clerk in Waldbaum's, someone she had known in high school, she was also getting him washed, dressed, and into his wheelchair. She expected Jamie to cooperate, and so he did. On Sunday nights, Jamie could hardly wait to pick up where the Fridays in Diane's life had left him off. (After Jamie died, Diane would stop working private duty cases.) Although I'd been up all through the night turning Jamie, it wasn't until Diane walked through the front door in the mornings that I was calm enough to feel exhausted. I was supposed to be working on a book—this book—but instead, when Diane was here, I slept on my bedroom floor, with my head under the desk, like George Costanza, the Jason Alexander character on *Seinfeld*. In that last year, someone was always telling me about the blue lint in my hair.

After Diane left, and on weekends during that last year, when Patrick or I sat next to Jamie in that rocking chair, he was frightened. Our own son, and because we weren't nurses, he was scared to be alone with us. "What if I start to choke?" he asked, "What if I can't breathe?" "You won't choke, we assured him," rubbing his back again in wide circles, though we had no idea what we'd do if he did. "You'll be able to breathe," we assured him, though we had no idea what we'd do if he couldn't. In that last year, at bedtime, when he was on the vent, in an expansive mood, not worried about breathing, he talked about the cheeseburger he was going to eat "tomorrow," as if he'd wake up and suddenly be able to swallow. Like anyone in a wheelchair for any length of time, he was tortured by constipation. While I was sitting right next to him rubbing his back, I was also, to my great shame, imagining him gone, neither Patrick nor I sitting in that rocking chair, but in the yard planting flowers, or sitting on the deck together reading *Newsday,* or going to Mass. And then I felt terrible. No Jamie to talk to, no Jamie to find the old Jamie inside of, no Jamie to rest his head on my shoulder all the way home from Patrick's house, where he was so frightened of choking that no food could tempt him. When Patrick Sr. sank to his knees in Patrick's Jr.'s bathroom, and almost dropped Jamie on the tile floor, I knew that things were ending. He'd been carrying muscular dystrophy boys in his arms for too many years—and it was getting to be too much, even for someone as strong as he.

"I guess I'll never have a girlfriend," Jamie said one hot afternoon as we drove to the movies, where, under safe cover of the dark, deserted theater, sitting side by side, one of the few experiences we could still share, I'd hold his icy cold hand in mine. I wanted him to know that I would never let him go, and so I touched him whenever I could, and it wouldn't embarrass him. When he could still steer his motorized wheelchair, there was nothing I liked more than walking alongside him with my arm resting on his shoulder—something I hadn't done with Patrick Jr. since he was a little boy—or my fingers brushing his forearm. If it was a story we had together, then these touches were the punctuation. "I guess not," I said, pulling down the old Star Wars shield, and staring straight ahead. "Given a choice," I once asked him, "would you rather have not been born?" "Yes," he said. Then he said, "No." Then, "I don't know." I wonder if that was the afternoon he sat at his computer, writing the thoughts I would accidentally stumble upon a year after his death:

> They say that ignorance is bliss, and if it's true, then my parents must have been the happiest couple who ever existed.
>
> Over and over again, I ask myself why they tempted fate, when their firstborn son was healthy, and had no abnormalities?
>
> They thought it was "reasonable" to try again, and instead

of being satisfied with what they had, they were trying an-other hand of Russian roulette—only they were playing with *my* chips. And the rest, as they say, is history.

And I'm paying for their gamble—but they aren't getting away cleanly, either, because they're stuck with me. It's a real nightmare for everyone involved. Our whole family has been royally screwed over by God, or some other cosmic, di-vine, "intelligence," or the aliens, who hold the answers to all of life's little mysteries.

And now it's time to pay the piper.

My cousins and I will suffer, get thinner, weaker, smaller, and quieter, when all we'll hear are ventilators, and respiratory equipment that will breathe for us, and help us live, if we're lucky, to the ripe old age of say—thirty.

Blame is the only commodity that's given out for free, and never wanted, but I can't blame my parents, my rela-tives, or anyone else for this wonderful "gift" that keeps tak-ing life from the living.

Many factors create a human being—mother's blood, fa-ther's blood, a baby's sex, hair color, eye color. Ridiculous for any one parent, or any one child, to lay guilt or blame on one single person for passing a birth defect to an innocent baby when both parents are involved.

But just because they love me, and want me to live, they won't let me go my own way, and get out of my way.

But he didn't tell me any of that.

He smiled at me, and changed the subject. "Hey," he said, "the sun is shining, we're going to see a new Spike Lee movie, and I took a dump. Life can be beautiful!"

One day when Jamie was a student at Suffolk Community College, his bus broke down and he needed a lift home. I drove the van to the campus, and sat on the library steps to wait. It was a bright, sunny day, and all around me were kissing, laughing, frisbee-tossing youngsters, a sea of kids in denim. I noticed how many of the boys had silky reddish hair like Jamie's, and how many of them, like Jamie, like my father, were slightly built. Whenever I saw Jamie with his peers, it was Patrick—broad across the back, massive through the shoulders—that I thought about. It was the only way I could get through it. Sitting in the sunshine, I had myself half convinced that it was all a dream, that the Jamie I was meeting wasn't the sick youngster he'd become, but the denim, vigorous, beautiful Jamie that could have been.

"Successful adaptation," Dr. John Bach writes in the *American Journal of Physical Medicine & Rehabilitation* of boys with muscular dystrophy, "does not depend on an accurate perception of reality."

Perhaps that goes for their mothers, too.

When the sea of denim parted, there was Jamie, wearing a sweatshirt and sweatpants, coming at me full speed ahead in his motorized wheelchair, proud of himself, and so happy to see me, while I was so deeply disappointed to see him, the flawed son my flawed body had created.

In Jamie's last year, with Diane or me at his side, he took an English course at Stony Brook, went to a few movies, and made some trips to Border's Books, where I had to drop the manual ramp, roll Jamie out, and leave him while I found a parking spot. When he was sitting right next to me, in a movie theater, or a classroom, it seemed entirely possible that he might indeed live to be thirty, but when I saw him from across the great asphalt gulf of parking lot, and watched the shoppers he was unaware of walking behind him nudging each other, gaping, or doing double takes, it didn't seem that he'd even live through the day. I couldn't bear to see it, and so when I turned the van off, I ran across the parking lot—and a woman not only of a certain age, but of a certain weight, dodging cars, and running through a parking lot, desperate to close a gap only she can see, is never a pretty sight—though it always made Jamie smile.

CHAPTER NINETEEN

HE FIRST NIGHT THAT JAMIE WAS GONE, I SLEPT IN my clothes. When I woke up, the bedroom was bright and sunny. Too many birds were singing in the yard. Except for water running in the kitchen sink, the house was quiet. I got out of bed, stuck my feet in my flip-flops, and stood up. I felt proud of myself. It was my first tiny yes.

I looked through the window, and was glad to see Patrick and Pat getting into the car and driving off somewhere. I didn't care where they were going. It was a relief not to wake up to both of them staring at me, as if they were expecting me to hit the rewind button, stop their hurt, bring Jamie back. After all, they seemed to be thinking, you were in charge of him for all those years—can't you do something? Only I couldn't. For seventeen of his twenty-four years, I'd been preparing for Jamie's death—why hadn't they?

In the kitchen, Nicole was washing dishes. Because it so obviously was her watch, I tried to act sane—although I didn't feel sane at all, breathing as if I'd just run the marathon, and the birds were driving me crazy. "I'm going to take a shower," I announced. Perhaps I shouted. Startled, Nicole turned from the stove. "Okay," she said, looking scared and staring uneasily at me and then at the coffee yogurt—my favorite—on the kitchen table, with a napkin, and a spoon, but I couldn't eat a thing.

When I opened the linen closet, looking for a towel, I saw it all—the pills, the nasal sprays, the boxes of ventilator tubing, the latex gloves, the Chux pads, the bedpans, the urinals, all the things that belong in a nursing home for the last days of long lives and not for the last days of someone twenty-four. I pulled everything out of the closet and dropped it onto the floor, kicking the bottles rolling around. "Are you alright?" Nicole called, but I couldn't answer her. I could barely breathe. *He was my life, my whole goddamn life.* So much for acting sane. On the floor of the linen closet were the extra batteries, big as car batteries—for the vent, for the extra vent, for the suction machine and the extra suction machine, for the wheelchair, and the extra wheelchair—plus the boat battery just in case any of them failed. I dragged them to the middle of the bathroom floor too. When there was no more room for me to move, I gathered the bottles of pills in my T-shirt, and yanked open the bathroom door. Nicole and I stood face to face. Without saying a word, she took the pills from my hands, headed for the front door, out to the garbage pail. Then Patrick and Pat came home with steaming cups of coffee that they left on the table when they came looking for me. In a sorry parade, the four of us dragged the batteries, the machines, the hoya lift, the commode chair, and the wheelchairs out of our small house and lined everything up on the porch, waiting for someone from the Muscular Dystrophy Association to stop by, and take it all away, the glittering chrome in the heartless spring sunshine for all the neighbors to see—even the commode chair, all out in the open, under the pretty blue suburban skies. Like Jackie Kennedy in that blood-stained suit, I wanted to push our war in my neighbors' innocent faces, what we were going through while they were outside mowing their lawns, worrying about the weeds, barbecuing their hamburgers, having company. While we watched their kids riding up and down on their bikes, while we heard them telling their kids to find their sneakers and get into the car, while they were heading to the sandy beaches that were off-limits to the wheelchair, or to the fast-food places for happy meals that Jamie couldn't swallow. I want them to see what we needed to keep Jamie alive, while they were asking how he was doing, and I was answering, "Hanging in there." I wanted them to see what "hanging in there" meant.

Though the four of us—Patrick, Pat, Nicole, and I—had never been in a car together, for we always had Jamie with us, and he could only ride in the van, we drove in one car to the funeral home. It was so odd to think that in life, Jamie had hardly gone anywhere without me, and yet, someone had taken him from the hospital to the funeral home, had brought him through the white side door of the funeral home that we must have driven past a hundred times, and never noticed. The undertaker had done his job beautifully. Just as in the hospital, Jamie looked as if he had another lifetime to go. If I looked down at him in a certain way, I could still see his blue eyes, though they were the glass eyes of a mannequin, and not Jamie's any longer. As he had done a million times in Jamie's life, Patrick Sr. adjusted his legs, feeling underneath for the thick oatmeal-colored Gap socks he'd brought to the undertaker. "He's still soft," Patrick said, smiling at me, happy that we still had Jamie, if only for a bit longer, on our half of the divide. At that moment, I'd never felt sorrier for anyone, or loved anyone more. Half a dozen times in the Stony Brook "Trauma/Critical Care Unit" there was always one moment when everyone—even Jamie, on the stretcher in front of us— seemed to fade away, and left Patrick and me staring into each other's eyes, as if we were about to dance. The last time we were there, on either side of Jamie's curtain were dead people wearing toe tags—and even *they* faded away when Patrick bent down and kissed the top of my head.

At the wake, I tried to be my mother's fine Irish daughter. Even though she was dead and buried, I wanted her to be proud of me. I kept my back ramrod straight, and my mouth razor sharp, with a ready arsenal of anecdote—although my timing was off, and nobody laughed. Until that last night, I almost pulled it off. But then I looked at Patrick, pale and sweaty, folded over too many shoulders, and Patrick Jr., his almost-military bearing, never leaving the foot of the casket, and my sister Pam, walking toward me with her arms out, and the chapel turning pin quiet, that finally did me in. For the moment, it was too much to bear. I bolted, ran out of the chapel and into the funeral home lobby. I hadn't counted on everyone in the room following me, in a crazy receiving line that snaked down the corridor, into the lobby, and into the parking lot.

"It's our *annus horribilis*," I said to whoever asked how we were doing. I didn't say that it was the strangest thing—though I hadn't carried Jamie in weeks, my arms ached anyway. *"Annus horribilis"* was what a dignified and stalwart Queen Elizabeth had said during the royal family's days of divorce/tragedy/humiliation. But since this is Long Island and not Leeds, nobody knew what I was talking about. Not the nice lady at the bank when I closed Jamie's account, not the mailman delivering all those heavy Mass cards, not the nice, Nordic-looking man who lived across the street, and when he saw me taking a walk through the neighborhood, always stopped to ask. He'd seen all the ambulances coming for Jamie, and he was on the lawn with the other neighbors the day that my mother died. I barely knew him, and he'd come to the same funeral home for us twice in one year. When I said *"annus horribilis,"* the Nordic-looking man seemed uncomfortable, as if I were complaining about hemorrhoids, and so I started saying "hanging in there" all over again. He seemed relieved. I didn't want to alienate the Nordic-looking man. Though people called me, on some days, at least until Patrick came home, the Nordic-looking man was the only person I met face to face. Loneliness had become a kind of yeast, and made my grief double in size. I found that putting my slippers on was only the tiniest part of "yes"—the next step was getting out of the house. It's companionship that forces grief into a smaller container, and makes it easier to carry.

CHAPTER TWENTY

J AMIE IS IN THE CATHOLIC CEMETERY, A FEW MILES down the road, the one we used to speed past on our way to Blockbuster Video. In the very beginning, my grief felt like Patrick Jr.'s birth, when the body I thought I knew so well, my body, traitor that it seemed to be, proved to be surprisingly capable of producing that much pain.

On our first visit to the cemetery, a day after the funeral, I laid face-down on the grave, until Patrick, in a fury, grabbed my hand, and pulled me to my unsteady feet, sticks and pebbles in my hair, and shook me like a child. I tried to hit him, but I missed, and instead, I pulled away from him and ran to the car, where I locked him out. He stood next to the car door, glaring at me, shaking his head, shaking his fist, yelling something I couldn't hear. That night there was a cold rain, I had to go to bed. You'd think we lived in sunny California with all the thought I'd given to cold rain. The shiny casket had felt so warm in the May sunshine. There's room for the three of us in the grave, and that's a consolation. We decided that Patrick

Jr.'s suggestion, "Till we meet again," is the perfect epigraph. Before the headstone was in place, the grave looked lumpy, like a poorly made bed, though in a way, it was comforting, in one glance, familiar to our family's "type"—the thick, bulky hem family, the emergency home haircuts family, the family with the forgotten cookies, soggy and crumbly in the bottoms of the schoolbags. Somebody took the small pair of white angels I'd bought at Odds n Ends in the Village, where I'd stood in line behind an old lady who, despite the warm day, had worn a green knit cap, telling anyone who would listen that the bud vase in her hand was for her microwave tea. The blue-eyed Romanian owner, who hates returns, and wants everyone to know exactly what they're buying, tried to dissuade her, grabbing a fake flower from a bin near the register and sticking it in the vase. "For this!" he sputtered, "For this!" But it was no use. "But will the tea bag fit?" the old lady asked, over and over again, until he gave up and sold it to her anyway. On either side of Jamie were tall, stern-looking red geraniums, who seemed to pull away from the eager, round pink snapdragons I planted after the angels disappeared—there goes the neighborhood. On windy days at the cemetery, I stood perfectly still under one small tree, watching sad little notes, yellowed greeting cards, and odd little toys blow through the rows of headstones like bewildered tourists.

In the beginning, I went to the cemetery every morning, and then I went home. An hour later, I drove to the supermarket and then I went home, to the beach and then I went home, to church and then home again just to fill the hours. Nothing felt familiar, nothing felt right. Wheelchairs attract attention, and whoever is in one, or behind one, plays a very public part. If you're not pushing the wheelchair, you're getting it into the massive van, tying or untying the tie-downs, and the chains, and the bolts, opening or closing the ramps. Though you're dressed like a workman, in your sensible sneakers and your jeans smudged with dirt from the wheelchair wheels, you're just one woman after all, climbing behind the wheel of that huge van, and someone, somewhere is always watching. Telling yourself that you're living the life that matters is the only thing that gets you through—but the sad fact is, that when it's over, you miss the attention. Suddenly, nobody's staring. Nobody sees your battle now, nobody sees your scars. Your "special-ness" is down the tubes. Now, you're just like everybody else, realizing what they already know, that living the "life that mat-ters" is a do-it-yourself proposition. Welcome to the real world. But in the mirror, my optimistic, "strong," and "can-do" wheel-chair face was the only one I recognized. It had been so long, I'd forgotten I'd ever had any other.

Patrick went to the cemetry after work, and we went to-gether on the weekends. Patrick didn't want a headstone just yet. "It makes it too permanent," he said, but it was the "tem-porariness" that drove me crazy. I was afraid that one of those mornings, I'd hear Jamie struggling to breathe. I needed the headstone, the finality of words. Instead of arguing about the headstone, we went to an expensive restaurant, ordered dinner and drinks, and toasted Jamie's well-lived, sliver of a life—only nothing was final at all. In the middle of our fancy dinner, we fell into missing him as one would fall into a well and couldn't finish—not the dinner, not the conversation. On the one-month anniversary, Patrick Jr. drove down, picked me up, and we headed for the cemetery where the grave next to Jamie's was open. That was unbearable. We jumped into the car and sped away.

When Pam came down, we sat on either side of the grave, our knees touching as if we were back in our old bedroom. "Give me half an hour," she said, "and a big spoon. I'll have him out of here in no time."

When Patrick saw that I'd put a child's pinwheel into the dirt, he raced home, threw open the screen door, stomped through the house, and into the yard where I was sitting underneath the big tree, and screamed that I was making Jamie a child when he was a twenty-four-year-old man, for Christ's sake, and I screamed back that a pinwheel attracts birds, and Jamie loved birds, and then we told each other unceremoniously to fuck off, burst into tears while holding each other until I pulled away, went inside to make us tea, and brought steaming mugs out to the deck. "How am I supposed to eat with my son in his grave?" is what I asked the kitchen wall one night, like "Shirley Valentine." I couldn't cook. Every meal I attempted reminded me of everything Jamie couldn't swallow. "He was my son, too," Patrick called from the living room. "And I can eat alright." He annoyed me beyond belief. To a patient, listening someone on the phone, I said, "I had to buy baby food for my grown son," and from the living room, I heard Patrick mutter, "Yeah, I bought the baby food too," and when I hung up, I turned to him, and screamed, "But he was more *my* son! You were at work! He was my goddamn *life*!"

"Did you want to *eat*?" he screamed. "*Someone* had to work!"

"Jamie *was* my work!" I screamed back.

Then we told each other to fuck off, held each other, and I made tea.

Although after Jamie died, we could sleep through the night again, something we hadn't done for seventeen years, we didn't. When one of us was restless, got up, went to the bathroom, the other was sitting up and wide-awake, putting on the light, and then the TV. We avoided the living room, where Jamie spent most of his time—especially in the middle of the night. It was as if the living room had a crater in its center, and we were afraid of falling in. "Are you alright?" we were forever asking each other, sometimes at the same time. In the beginning, Patrick Jr. called us every few hours. My normal son. Sometimes, it seemed to me as if Jamie had spent his short life sitting in a circle of golden light, on some sort of a stage, and I'd been in the first row. Offstage, there was much slamming of doors, Patrick Jr. coming in and out with schoolbooks, friends, hockey sticks, basketballs—and then, one day, I looked up, and he was walking through the door in a tuxedo, leaving to get married. Sounding so small on the phone, Patrick said he didn't remember his father hugging and kissing him as much as he did since "it" happened, and though he was worried about us, he was too upset to visit. He said he didn't want to be the only child. He said it was killing him that he wouldn't have his brother to grow old with. I sat up straight in my chair, and told him—as if a parent could replace a sibling—that I was only twenty years older than he was, that the chances were good that I would be around for a very long time, and as long as there was breath in my body, I'd be here for him. "It seems to me that life is pretty pointless," he said, "you might as well just throw yourself in front of a train," and then I got angry. *"How dare you!"* I screamed, *"How dare you say that to someone who has just buried their other child? What gives you that right?"* And then Patrick, who had no idea what Patrick had said, grabbed the phone from me, and then *he* started screaming: *"How dare you upset your mother like that?"* and then the three of us were crying, and when we hung up, Patrick and I staggered into bed. In the morning, I woke with a new purpose—writing a letter to Patrick Jr. I told him that his father and I were creating a new marriage, that Jamie's loss had brought us closer together, that we were devoted to him and Nicole, that Patrick and I were healthy, capable, here for each other—all the things that I hoped, in time, would come true, and while I was writing, I was seeing both of them in the bathtub, their roundness, their light-as-air hair, their ears, necks, feet. Muscular dystrophy, you son of a bitch. Jamie's loss was dividing us into camps of who was hurting more. At times, the "new marriage" felt much harder than the old one. In the old marriage, I would never have left Patrick frantically wandering through the aisles of Home Depot calling my name while I was outside, sitting in the car. A few days later, again on the phone, Patrick Jr. told me that he had cracked a joke for the first time since his brother died, and he felt he had "turned the corner," and I said I was glad to hear that. I wish I had told him that in the city of grief there is no one corner. There are a bunch of corners, and you have to keep turning them again and again. As many farewells, Shakespeare wrote, as the stars in heaven.

But Patrick Sr. didn't want to talk about Jamie. "He's happy where he is," he said, as if Jamie were at Club Med, or "He's free from his suffering," and then he went into the yard to mow the grass, or play with the dog, whom I'd begun to detest. Life wasted on a dog—though he was Jamie's dog, and the dog gave Jamie a lot of pleasure. Still, I wasn't appeased. "Jamie's Dog" could have been the title of some cheesy, after-school special. "It's selfish of us to long for him," Patrick said, rational all the way to his engineering soul, "his life was so hard," "Yadda, yadda," I said. "But don't you wonder if he misses us?" I asked Patrick once, when we were in the car, and he was driving, with no lawn, no dog, no escape. "Don't you just want to hear him say, 'I'm here, and it's great?'" "No," Patrick said, and handed me a tissue from the box of funeral parlor tissues still in the car. "I know he's there—wherever 'there' is. He's in heaven," he said, and then I wanted to hit Patrick again. "He just couldn't live anymore," Patrick said, shrugging his shoulders, "why can't you just accept it?" I didn't know why. I just couldn't. All the funeral food was finally out of the refrigerator, but there seemed to be no end to the tears, or the box of funeral parlor tissues.

So we went to fast-food places as though they were gin mills or crack houses. Trying not to slip on greasy napkins and pick-up sticks straws, we stood at fast-food counters and ordered greasy foods Jamie couldn't swallow from freckled-faced teenagers wearing paper hats. In a way it was reassuring. The cemetery where we spent so much time was too full of young people. What we needed at the fast-food places was not so much instant food as instant youngsters. When they gave us our change, and we drove away with grease-splattered paper bags, we felt better. Then we got fat. The tiny chins that fit our small faces were lost in our large, loose faces, spare tires not only around our waists, but also around our necks, and when we screamed at each other, our jowls swung like hammocks.

Fast-food dinners, and running from the crater waiting for us at home, we ran to the movies where we passed the bank of telephones, but there was no nurse to call to see how he's doing. I missed the nurses. I'd never know if Pauline's son ever made her a grandmother, if Anne ever bought a better house, if Linda's husband stayed cancer-free, if Diane ever married Warren. All I have left of the nurses are their handwritten recipes on index cards in my flowered recipe box. I missed Kenny the respiratory technician who made house calls and was about to have his first baby, Shirley in the drug store who brought me to the head of the line for Jamie's useless medicines, Doreen, the beautiful physical therapist whose son wanted to be a writer. It was sad to realize I'd never know how any of it turned out.

Telephone calls. How was I doing? Oh, I was just swell. I couldn't leave the house without my notebook, into which I wrote what I was supposed to do, where I was supposed to go and I was so crazy that at stop lights, I had to check the notebook to see what to do next. I even brought my notebook with me to Mass, and when I left my seat to take Communion, left it in the pew, hoping some of the friendly people in church would open it, see how upset I am, invite me back to their houses for a cup of tea. When I got to where I was going,

I felt like I was going to faint. Everything turned white, and I got a sweet, sickish taste in my mouth. My attention span was like a puppy, and needed to be led to the next thing. When a friend called to say hello, and told me what a fortune-teller she'd just been to had predicted for her children: fame, fortune, happiness forever, I was barely able to stand it. "That's good," I said. I had a second set of holes pierced through my ears, and I bought a pair of earrings in Jamie's birthstone: sapphire. They hurt when I talked on the phone but I didn't care. Isn't it the drive to push away psychic pain that makes people mutilate themselves? "What's wrong?" a friend asked, the minute I picked up the phone. "But sweetheart, you know that Jamie is happy," she said. I pictured her messy kitchen, her big house packed with children, dogs, sneakers in a jumble by the door, a dozen towels drying on the line. "You know that he wouldn't want you to be sad." "I just miss him," I said. "Well, of course you do," she says, oblivious. Some who called cut me off, midsentence. "But look at your poor sister!" they said, "with two of them!" Nobody seems to remember who is older, or even what my nephews' names are, or consider that what I feel for them might be what they feel for their own healthy nieces and nephews. And of course, they were right. Two sons with muscular dystrophy are much, much worse than one, but that doesn't make me feel any better. It was Victor Frankl, the Holocaust survivor, who wrote that grief is like a gas that fills whatever container it inhabits. It was Jamie I was grieving—Chris and Jason were still alive. Others called, and it was a relief to hear about their sister Margaret's sinus trouble, or their transmission, or the new bedroom furniture they'd seen at the mall. They didn't have to know what to say, but I was so glad to hear from them anyway. "I'm sorry for your trouble" is what Irish kids hear at all those wakes, and that's about as good as it gets.

It's the "misery loves company" callers that I could really do without. All the cancer, all the heart attacks, all the dropping dead stories didn't make me feel any better but much much worse. I was looking for reasons to say "yes," not to cash the whole damn thing in.

And then there were people three and four times Jamie's age who seemed to be everywhere, humped over, yet refusing to take the gravitational hint. In the church parking lot, and in the supermarket, I walked past knots of old people with eyes so lively and bright, you'd look at them, and think they won the lottery—but when I listened, the three little words that made me either jump into my car and pull away so fast, I scraped the side of the rectory, or walk right past the broccoli, and the hell with it anyway, buy Fritos and chocolate-covered pretzels. I told myself I was just too neurotic for grief. For the longest time, getting back in the living room after a walk to the mailbox felt like a great achievement, and made me want to plant the American flag in a sofa cushion.

CHAPTER TWENTY-ONE

T HOUGH I DIDN'T KNOW HOW TO GO ABOUT IT, AND each and every day felt like a desert I had to cross while wearing ice skates and a woolen coat (and Naugahyde knickers and a wooden hat, like the punchline from the old seventies joke), I set out deliberately to get better. With Jamie and my mother gone, I'd lost some of my future, and all of my past. Like care-taking, writing is a lonely, isolating business, and I had no wide circle of friends, or interests, or job, to go back to. Patrick and I were the over-extended parents of a very young child, so dependent on us that he made us young parents again. You give life to normal children, and they pretty much take it from there. But handicapped children, on the other hand, need so much that day after day after day, they are constantly re-created—but their parents are constantly re-created too. Patrick Jr. was off into the world, but Jamie kept us "Mommy" and "Daddy," and he was our perennial little boy.

Pam was busy with the boys. Patrick was at work all day,

and Pat Jr. and Nicole were back to living their Connecticut life. Though it took me awhile, I finally realized that recovering from grief—like the life that matters—is also a do-it-yourself proposition.

Ruthie has been my best friend for forty years, and her house, which I secretly think of as a repair shop for broken people, is where I began. It seemed as good a place as any. The guy whose wife threw him out lived for awhile in Ruth and Tony's basement, and so did the troubled kids with nowhere else to go, loose in the neighborhood on Thanksgiving Day, and Christmas, who found a place at Ruth and Tony's table, and a package underneath the tree. Even a huge, stray dog snuck in, and stole a meatloaf from the dinner table. When Ruthie looked up from the kitchen table where she was reading *Newsday,* and saw me standing in the doorway, "like a drop-in, normal person," she said, we both cried. I knew exactly what she meant—I was no longer wild-eyed, red-faced, or frantically hovering over Jamie, and he was no longer dissolving right in front of us. Ruth and Tony had seen it all too. It was in their yard that four-year-old Jamie climbed on top of the old redwood table, stood up, took the plastic bowl of ice cream Ruthie offered him, and shrieked "Grown-ups are terrific!"

But once I was there, in my new, Jamie-free life, I couldn't do much more than stand in the doorway, like some Thornton Wilder's Emily. Ruth and Tony have four kids, and their exuberance sometimes makes the walls shake, as if a constant earthquake were rumbling through the rooms. It was as though I needed to hold onto the doorframes to keep from soaring through the ceiling. It was too noisy. I was too fragile. There was too much going on. I told myself that I needed quiet, and so, I forced myself into the car, and drove three hours to Pam's house in Connecticut, ignoring my palpitating heart and the urge to scream, do a 360 on the highway, pull out all my hair. When I got to my sister's house, I headed straight for the couch. Though it was summer, I was freezing. She covered me with a thick white blanket and let me sleep.

A day or so later, in Pam's big kitchen, with its cinnamon walls, yellow and violet curtains, we stood at the stainless steel sinks, washing the razor-sharp cusinart blades and the strainer, and the particularly vicious-looking innards of the new, European puree machine. I was her future. She was my past. While we were working, there wasn't much to say. At Pam's house, necessity keeps the feelings at bay. She'd feed Chris, who's twenty-seven, and I'd feed Jason, who's twenty-six. Or vice versa. One of us will wash a face, move a foot, adjust an elbow. On the counter all around us are the accoutrements both of illness, and of health. Vancenese and organic tomatoes, Vasotec and bran muffins, Digoxin and strawberries, black and soft at the sides where they never made it to the refrigerator. When I visit my sister, there's the bright spot of time between us, a "DMZ" that muscular dystrophy can't touch, when she shows me her black-and-white photographs of what her artist's eye finds in the boys' faces, or the amazing Connecticut countryside, or I read her some of what I've written, or sometimes, we talk about God. It doesn't matter how many blades we wash in the sink, how many mouthfuls of food we give the boys. That bright spot is worth waiting for, and it's what that muscular dystrophy gave us.

Christopher doesn't like to leave the house, but Jason does, and when I'm there, I drive the two of us to the movies in their van. More movies. Movies with Richie, movies with Jamie, movies with Jason. Like Richie, like Jamie, Jason was an English major in college. My formal education can fill a thimble, and so Jason tells me about Shakespeare, and the allegory of *Star Trek,* and how he hates the Catholic church, which he knows I love, and will unsuccessfully defend, and he's talking so much that I find myself lost in ideas, and drive right past the exit. It's the middle of the afternoon, and I'm talking to my nephew, and it's straight from my soul, and straight from his. How many aunts and nephews get to know one another this deeply? And that's what muscular dystrophy gave us, too. It's almost as though I've gotten Jamie back. In the early days after Jamie died, when I visited Pam, I couldn't sleep, and sat on the side of the guest room bed. *What if Jamie's back,* I asked myself, *but in Jason's body?* And then the ghost of my mother inhabited the flowered chair across from me. "For Christ's sake, Christine," she says, "knock it off, willya?"

And yet when I get Jason out of the van, and am walking alongside him, it takes all the restraint I can muster not to wrap my arm around his shoulders, or touch his arm, or even stop walking for a few minutes so I can nuzzle him as I've seen my sister do, or brush my lips across the top of his head. It's the closest I can come to living Jamie's and my story once again. Or maybe it's the story I had with Richie. It's hard to tell the players without a scorecard. There are too many lost boys. Gentle, soothing, Christopher, an aspirin for the whole sore world, and funny, poetic Jason are the only ones left. I loved them all so. When I get home, it takes me days to sew up the tear in my heart, and the only way I can do it is with my notebook, and a pen. I ache for them. Richie, Jamie, Jason, Chris—even the lost boys I never knew.

Everyone told me that I needed a job, but until the afternoon that I found myself Scotch-taping red leaves to my living-room window, I didn't listen. I agreed that I needed a distraction, and yes, maybe for the first time in my life, writing wasn't enough. I imagined myself in a hot office, standing under the fluorescent lights searching for the Widdleman contract, which was last seen on Stacy's desk, underneath the Foogle papers, going stark raving mad. "Not a big deal job," everyone said, probably alarmed at the wild look in my eyes (I wanted to say that Jamie was my "big deal job"), "just a reason to get up, get dressed, get out of the house." "They're right," Patrick said, looking up from the sports pages. "You've been in the house for a very long time. You should do something you enjoy." Ah, there's the rub. I was so sad that there was little I enjoyed. The novel I published in 1992, before Jamie got so sick, belonged to another lifetime. "Well, something writing-ish," Pam said, and that's how I found myself, a bereaved mother of only a few months, wearing a denim dress, and sitting in the tiny editorial office of the *Long Island Advance* in Patchogue Village, Long Island, applying for a job as a newspaper reporter. School board meetings (Halloween contests, hotdogs vs. macaroni and cheese for lunch, and the science fair) and Village Hall meetings where the local businessmen had an open forum (parking meters vs. no parking meters, when to hang the Christmas lights on Main Street), sewing the hole in my heart this time with a steno book, and a pen. And it worked. It got me out of the house, and proved to be a blessing. Writing will save you, someone smart once told me—even if it is in tiny incremental amounts.

And then one balmy night, the undertaker who had "undertaken" not only Mom, but Jamie, stood up to speak. I don't remember what he said. The steno book slid from my lap. I couldn't do anything but stare at his hands. His hands, his hands . . . the gestured at the ceiling, gritty with dead flies, where the blades of the ceiling fan cut through the still air. We left the Village Hall at the same time. He recognized me and put his hand on my back. "How're you doing?" he asked, and it was all I could do not to grab his hands, kiss them, fall back into his arms.

In John Irving's novel *A Prayer for Owen Meany*, the title character says that people die little by little, until you can no longer remember their scent, their touch, their voices, their faces. It's probably true but to me, it seems that people die over and over again. Jamie dies when I look at his toothbrush— although I can't bring myself to throw it out—and he dies again whenever he gets any mail—for awhile there, more than when he was alive. He dies when a ridiculous new television show premieres, he dies when Jerry Springer makes a movie. He dies when I watch those car crash specials we used to watch together, when Oprah Winfrey and Maya Angelou are on TV in their pajamas, when Spike Lee, whom Jamie loved, directs another movie. On Friday nights, he dies all over again, when I come home from coffee with Ruthie to find Patrick curled up by himself on the couch, rather than curled up around Jamie in Jamie's hospital bed. He dies all over again when I get up in the middle of the night, and find nothing in his bedroom but the sickly blue light of his astronomy clock. Day moves onto day like those striped wax candles that melt onto themselves, and time, in its own sweet pace, repairs what is rent. It's been almost six years, and yet I think of him almost all the time. At first, the world was quiet and dark, but now, it's noisy and at times, much too bright. In the brightness, and the din, I can sometimes feel his presence, suddenly remembering how small his hands and feet were, how blue his eyes, how deep his dimples, and then I buy stamps, shoes, or lettuce harder than I did before, if such a thing is possible. Books, a bakery bag of warm corn muffins, dangling, new silver earrings are islands of comfort, and there are islands everywhere I look. Like the Tom Hanks character in *Cast Away,* not only is it a lot of effort to get back to the mainland, but I'm not sure I ever will. Like the Tom Hanks character, I'm changed forever. The difference is that I'm not alone. I'm trying hard, but dear reader, so are you.

Einstein said that there were two ways to live: as if nothing were a miracle, or as if everything is. I still spend miserable days in the first way, but now I live mostly in the second. Jamie's over there, in the cemetery, and behind him, a pair of baby boy twins, who didn't have muscular dystrophy, but lived only one day. Perhaps that day was filled with struggle, or perhaps not. Perhaps those tiny boys went from someplace safe and warm to someplace else safe and warm, with a brief stopover in their parents' arms, and are together, like my young uncles, for all eternity. Who's to say that one day wasn't perfect? A drive to the cemetery is a good way to forget the dry cleaner ruining your blouse, or the neighbor who snubbed you, or your sniffly little cold. When I visit, I look at all the headstones, and wonder what any of those souls would do with just one more day, the same day that's been given so quietly, so miraculously, and so generously to me.

Patrick says that Jamie is no longer there, and I guess he is right. In hopes that he lives on, in grass, and rain, and wind, and snow, I turn my face to the elements, icy rain pelting my cheeks, my tongue sticking out when nobody's looking, hoping for hail to bounce into my mouth.

"Never never quit," Churchill said, and he was right.

But I prefer to listen to my mother.

"Survive," the late, great Helen Doyle said, "you must survive."

I will, Mom. I promise I will.

CHAPTER TWENTY-TWO

UR GRANDDAUGHTER, ALANNA NICOLE, WAS BORN two days after the second anniversary of Jamie's death, on an overcast, drizzly May Monday. It was our third ferry ride to Connecticut in less than a week—the other trips had been false alarms. Parenthood hadn't come easily to Patrick and especially Nicole, who'd spent nearly half of her pregnancy lying flat on her back. Everyone was afraid that Alanna might be very early, though as it happened, she was just about on time. Though we didn't know it yet, by the time the ferry docked at Bridgeport, Patrick and I were grandparents. I'd like to think that at the moment of Alanna's birth, the waters of the Long Island Sound parted a bit, there was some movement on the Richter scale, or at the very least, we somehow just *knew*, but the truth of the matter was that the water had been rough, we'd scarfed down pretzels and warm soda instead of a proper dinner, and at the exact moment of the baby's birth, we were probably standing at the ferry rail, hoping they wouldn't come back up. Plus which we were freezing. On the shore, it might have been May but on the water, and inside of us, it was still November.

But then we got to the hospital, and Patrick Jr. was running down the corridor toward us. When they saw him coming, a pair of nurses had to split apart and hug the walls or be seriously flattened. It was only two years later that we three were back in the corridor of a hospital, but this time everything was different. This time, Patrick and I were semihysterical with joy, and Patrick Jr. was so ecstatic, he practically leapt into our arms. One at a time, he brought us through the nursery and to the side of Alanna's isolette. There she was, on her back, sound asleep, a big beautiful baby wearing nothing but a diaper and a cap. Though she was very pink, something about her was silvery too, as if, on her way to us, she might have brushed against the stars. When I held her for the first time, the baby was only a few hours old. Though Nicole was exhausted, had blood under her fingernails, and a smudge of blood across her right cheek, she pointed to the baby's long fingers, and said they reminded her of Jamie's. I was so grateful to Nicole, who'd so generously brought my baby into the room with us while I was holding hers. With my new granddaughter in my arms, I could feel myself soften, as if the grief I had for Jamie finally stood up, and offered the new baby its seat. Before I handed the baby to Patrick, I pressed her against my chest, hoping that my battered heart might somehow strengthen hers, and I kissed the top of her head. When we pulled into our driveway on that apricot-tinted dawn, the worst of it was over for us. Like Kafka's famous description of a book, our granddaughter was the ax to break the frozen sea within.

She wasn't yet two when she was sitting on my lap looking at family pictures, pointing to pictures of Jamie in his wheelchair, and looking up at me expectantly. "Uncle Jamie," I said, for I knew she was asking me *What's up with THIS?* but I didn't know quite what to say for after all, she was not yet two. When she *was* two, and we were all visiting Pam, Charlie, and the boys in Connecticut, she asked her Cousins Chris and Jason to get up out of their wheelchairs. "We can't," they said. "Why?" she wanted to know. "Because they have muscular dystrophy," I said, but as soon as the words were out of my mouth, I wanted to cut out my tongue. "Weak muscles" would have done just as well. For the first time, I understood that photo of my uncles in back of my grandmother's closet. I didn't want those terrible words near Alanna. I felt as though I were initiating this beautiful, innocent child into our terrible club, sharing a story she should have been spared. I guess I thought she wouldn't notice the wheelchairs in the photo album, or the wheelchairs in front of her. I wanted her to be unaffected by the whole thing, and not realize that muscular dystrophy had taken anything away from her father, from her grandparents, from *her*. We'd already given the damn thing too much. I didn't want Alanna's innocence to be yet another casualty of the muscular dystrophy war.

For the longest time, all I wanted to think about was how much muscular dystrophy had taken from me. It made my grandmother a hypochondriac, and made her afraid to leave the house. Even as the attendants were rolling her into the ambulance, she was plucking at their sleeves, and asking for "the boys" who had died some forty-three years before. Muscular dystrophy made my mother an only child, just as it has Patrick Jr., and a nervous wreck. She'd lost her brothers, she'd lost her son. She said she couldn't survive losing a grandson to the goddamn thing, and she didn't, and if there was a kindness to be found along the way for Mom, that was surely it. It took my father, the well of grief inside of him already filled to the brim. It took Richie, it took Jamie, it's taking Chris and Jason. It left a huge hole in our family's life. But if nature abhors a vacuum, then maybe that hole was what left room for other things. In a roundabout way, maybe it was muscular dystrophy that gave us the homemade rice pudding, the stories, our mother's adoration, and a love that made us surer in the world than we might have been otherwise.

Maybe it was through muscular dystrophy that we saw each other's strengths, as if we were looking at each other through 3-D glasses from the movies of the fifties. Everything that wasn't muscular dystrophy—like the old joke about the man who bangs his head because it feels so good when it stops—looked better, sounded better, tasted better, was much more fun. Very early on, I learned that the body—even a healthy body—is a fragile thing, and it's all about spirit anyway, just like the theologians say. It was Richie first, and then Jamie, who taught me that laughing in the face of muscular dystrophy was a way of fighting back. I watched my mother and I learned how to make home the best, when to make tea, how to endure. Muscular dystrophy wounded my father so deeply that I grew up determined to avoid his solution. When I was eleven, it was my mother who filled the prescription for a liquid tranquilizer that the doctor had ordered for me, and then handed it to me. "You have two choices," she said to me, "you can get through this hard life depending on medicine, or you can get through it depending on yourself. What's it gonna be?" and it was my mother who smiled when I poured it down the sink. I didn't want to learn any of these damn things. I wanted to have Richie for my sister and me to grow old with, and I wanted him to marry and have children, and I wanted him with us for the rest of our days, for the three of us were simpatico, but that wasn't the way it turned out. None of these lessons did I want, and yet I learned them anyway, bit by bit, in life's slow class, where they had the thick pencils.

I'm not sure that you come back from grief stronger, wiser, tougher, or purer in spirit. Part of you, especially when you lose a child, comes back crazy. These days, Patrick and I are like a couple of helium balloons, keeping each other out of the trees. When we get up at night for a drink of water, we say "I love you" to each other, and when we go anywhere, we hold hands. Sometimes, we make Patrick Jr. sick. We tell too many people we love them too, and we cry much too easily. If you see us coming, and you want to run the other way, we completely understand. But it's nothing we can help. It's what muscular dystrophy forced on us. To me, it all seems a miracle—Patrick Jr. walking up a flight of stairs, Alanna running along the sidewalk. You can keep your Botox—I'm happy to feel age rising in me like mercury through a thermometer. I'm happy to be still here. In restaurants, I'm delighted to watch everyone swallow, and I'm delighted to follow the natural rise and fall of a sleeping chest. With all those years in the house, I learned the most amazing thing, that you could sit perfectly still on your own front porch, or your living room, living a tiny life with a tiny circle of friends, and have one story after another walk up to you, tip its hat, be pleased to make your acquaintance. I learned how deep a life can be made from few ingredients and how futile a thing it is to live like an air traffic controller, holding a flashlight, bringing everyone you love through the snow, the fog, the hurricanes. Thank you, muscular dystrophy, for so much of what I know. Some days, the pain of losing Jamie feels like a boulder on my chest, and on other days, a pebble that sinks to the bottom of my shoe, or on other days lodges in my tooth. Which tooth? Doesn't matter. Once I zero in on it, it's in my eye, or up my nose, or rolling around in my ear. The hurt is always with me. Beautiful days are tinged with a brilliant, hard sadness, as if each day Jamie won't see is behind an unbreakable glass. My loss, my regret, color the seasons in a different way. Though it's sometime a log, and sometimes a matchstick, muscular dystrophy taught me that everyone is carrying something, and at any minute, one could be swapped for the other.

I look into the faces of twenty-two-year-old women, the age I was when Jamie was conceived, and I'm amazed not only that twenty-two is that hopeful, and that young, but that part of me is still twenty-two, ready to dance on the tables, and laugh at my own jokes. Joy is attached to our hearts with the most tenacious of threads.

It took nearly six years for Jamie to let go of me, the windows of my soul wide open, the floors "broom clean," the door softly shut behind him. Although he might have been "too ordinary" for all that was asked of him, the truth was that he became heroic.

Last winter, I was on Main Street, in Patchogue Village, picking my way across the ice in slippery shoes when an old man with a package in his arms stopped me. I wanted to keep going, for I was afraid he was about to fall, have a coronary, or a stroke (this is the part that comes back crazy), but what he wanted to tell me was that he'd just bought himself a nice coffeemaker for only sixteen dollars, and he'd gotten quite a bargain. That his wife had been dead for seventeen months, and he was surviving was the real story, his "understory," something he threw in before we parted. "Understories" are suddenly everywhere I look, and that's another of muscular dystrophy's gifts.

It's warm for December, and Alanna and I are in Peppermint Park, on the swings. She is on my lap, facing me. She's three years old, lives on Long Island now, and she knows how to pump. We're pumping so hard, I tell her we're going to touch the stars. "I know how we can get Uncle Jamie home for Christmas," she yells, though I can hardly hear her, we're swinging so fast. "How?" I ask. "First, we cut his arms open, and we take out the weak," she yells. "Then, we cut his legs open, and take out the weak. Then we take out his heart, and we fix it, and we put it back. Then we get a big, strong rope, and we tie it around him, and we pull him down from heaven. Then he can be home for Christmas!"

I don't know what to say, and so I just smile back at her. She's so small, and she's all she has.

"Higher, Bammy!" she squeals, "I want to go to the stars!" and there we are, about ready to fly into space. When she's older, I'll tell her that the elements in her body began in the stars, and if she just follows the sparks in her life, she'll know just where to go—but not now. Now I just hold her tight, and think of Lily Tomlin's line: "We're all in this together, by ourselves."

1. This book is a true story of one family's struggle with a fatal disease—and a carefully crafted narrative. What are some of the techniques that O'Hagan used to create characters that involve us deeply in her story?

2. Why did O'Hagan choose to present her son Jamie's death scene in the prologue? Do you agree with the decision to begin the memoir on such an intense note?

3. Though this memoir is sad, it is also funny. What impact does humor have on your experience of the book?

4. During much of the book, O'Hagan grapples with her desire for "a life that matters." Discuss whether her desire was fulfilled.

A Reading Group Guide

5. In several emotionally charged passages, the author describes the grief that she and her husband experienced right after their son's death. Will this memoir be helpful for parents who suffer the ultimate loss?

6. O'Hagan doesn't credit her Catholic faith or any one source of strength as the "magic bullet" that carried her through. Instead, she writes about following "sparks." What does this say about her religious upbringing? What do you find helpful when confronting life's hardships?

7. The author writes about muscular dystrophy's "gifts." Discuss the idea that difficult circumstances can offer gifts.

8. Though begun on a sad note, the book ends optimistically with the author at the playground with her three-year-old granddaughter. O'Hagan writes that "joy is attached to our hearts with the most tenacious of threads." Discuss whether this statement resonates with your own life experiences.

For more reading group suggestions visit
www.stmartins.com/smp/rgg.html

St. Martin's
Griffin